ConsumAuthors

Francesco Morace

B
U
P

The New Generational Nuclei

Original Title: ConsumAutori
Copyright © 2016 EGEA S.p.A.

Translation: Giovanni A. Viscomi
Typesetting: Laura Panigara, Cesano Boscone (MI)

Copyright © 2017 Bocconi University Press
EGEA S.p.A.

EGEA S.p.A.
Via Salasco, 5 - 20136 Milano
Tel. 02/5836.5751 – Fax 02/5836.5753
egea.edizioni@unibocconi.it – www.egeaeditore.it

First Edition: January 2017

ISBN International Edition 978-88-85486-00-3
ISBN Domestic Edition 978-88-99902-00-1
ISBN Mobypocket Edition 978-88-85486-02-7
ISBN Epub Edition 978-88-85486-01-0

Print: Digital Print Service, Segrate (MI)

Table of Contents

Foreword

by *Massimiliano Valerii*[*] and *Francesco Maietta*[**]

There are beliefs that are timeless. They endure, despite being rejected by the social behaviours of millions of people, especially when they take the form of moralistic epithets. The demonization of consumption is one such belief, often relegated it to a pathological practice where material objects reign over man through perverse commodification.

However, the economic crisis of 2008 brought changes to the age of compulsive consumerism. Today, the relentless drive for ever-greater growth according to the logic that "more is always better," allows us to look at the profound relationship we have with consumption with a fresh perspective, and discover its true social and collective meaning.

This book by Francesco Morace offers a powerful contribution to such a pertinent theme, primarily because it chooses an approach – that of the generational nuclei – that places us in a privileged position to analyse and interpret the processes. The fact that, today, different generations are no longer in open conflict, allows us to retrace the essential components of our social behaviours.

The classification of generational nuclei is not a marketing gimmick, but a vital interpretative tool that allows us to focus on the dynamics destined to shape the future. It is a courageous piece of social research that allows us to find a tangible reference point in a reality that has become fluid, elusive and non-compliant to pre-established patterns. The methodological choice also allows us to follow the flow of phenomenology with-

---

[*] Director General Fondazione Censis.
[**] Responsible Social Policies Fondazione Censis.

out being trampled upon, to form interpretations standing on the crest of the waves; for this reading the text proves the best option.

The generational and phenomenological approach are essential to interpret a context in which the power of subjectivity rules. This push towards individual freedom has choice as its primary form of expression. From food and clothing to holidays, what Morace calls "personal and family networks [...] the creative diversity of each and everyone" dominates.

In this way, consumption is freed from its negative pathological connotations of compulsion and excess with overflowing pantries and wardrobes. Instead, it becomes re-defined as a vehicle of wellbeing, values and relations; sobriety marks the new paradigm of choices and consumption patterns geared towards discernment, selection and sustainability.

The rhetoric of impersonal consumerism, that undermines values and controls minds, gives way to consumption as an expression of individuality in the broadest sense, of values and expectations, of people in relation to others and the context in which they live. By fighting against clichés and false prophecies, Morace helps us to understand that consumption in the era of neo-sobriety can be a 'good growth' and the only alternative to degrowth.

The strength of mature subjectivity generates new opportunities and is also likely to define the sense of place, with smart and individual use of contexts. Morace cleverly demonstrates the fate of these so-called non-places that for too long have been seen as depersonalizing contexts, devoted to turning individuals into clones of compulsive consumers. Instead they are increasingly the scenes of a multiple uses by different generations that fill them with their original, subjective meaning: relationships between adolescents, the location of family leisure time, or the everyday life of many elderly individuals. Indeed, the idea of shopping malls that some naively imagine as sterile places, emptied of humanity and only spaces for consumption junkies, is disproved.

On the other hand, people's attention to the distinctiveness of local products and places increases. For food, this reaches its highest point with the demand for traceability. However, it is a constitutive component in purchasing and consumption choices in all sectors. We want to learn the history of what we consume: the real origin, the stories of the communities involved, the environmental and social trace left in its path. If such information is not provided we search for it with dogged stubbornness. We no longer want to be anonymous consumers of ever cheaper, homogenised and interchangeable products without history, but mature and aware individuals able to bend consumption to our constellation of values, tastes and preferences.

Although not yet the materialization of 'power to the people', this is proof that some of the structural factors of Italian development are far from obsolete. It can start from the idea that change can only come from the grassroots, an intentional expression of millions of people who explain their own subjectivity and transform actions in the direction of improving their condition.

If this unleashing of these forces that generated the great saga of Italian development; that extraordinary journey to wealth and prosperity that marked Italy's post war history until the recent economic crisis. Today we need to take advantage of the new signs of potential growth, a growth that is able to make people happy by empowering them to change their lives for the better.

The reading of the phenomena and the unveiling of commonplaces perhaps paves the way for the book's most valuable contribution: the strength of individuals, and their ability to penetrate objects and contexts, and so indelibly marking the course of growth completed in relational value. It is in relationships with others that we express our individual identity, the true alternative to traditional hierarchical communities, open to those who escape from traditional bonds, and that stand as the "great protagonists of a large number of hopefully satisfactory relations [...where] personal happiness is also a direct consequence of the nature and quality of these relations."

Here we see the true value of Francesco Morace's analysis: the strength of subjectivity has historically changed the lives of Italians and has established itself in every sphere as the enzyme of growth and change, followed by pathological twists – from consumption to the deregulation of individual behaviours –, but able to take note of degeneration and limits, transforming the latter into a new strength, taking on behaviours based on values and practices of social and environmental sustainability. This mature and conscious subjectivity perceived in a relational nature at every level, is an unavoidable mechanism of self-realization. Thus, the multiplication of platforms and networks of relationships becomes the most formidable tool for growth and a higher quality of individual and community life.

In this guise, the Internet is not a tool that crystallizes distance between isolated monads, but a vehicle for a new sociality, that brings together, combines, generates, exchanges and creates new combinations, and, as a result, stimulates and promotes change.

Perhaps the secret to a new happy growth is here: following the era of the erosion of social and cultural ties operating as boulders of containment for individual freedom, we are now in an era of relationships between people and communities, which facilitates and completes individual freedom, becoming a multiplier of the strength of the individual.

From this perspective, the book is a pleasant and surprising guided tour to a future that is already here.

Preface. Beyond liquidity, Degrowth and non-places

The ConsumAuthor concept marks a new role for people in the dynamics of purchasing, and liberates consumption from the alleged demons of consumerism. The ConsumAuthors of all generations are individuals aware of their everyday choices. They free consumption from the negative and distorted characterisations espoused by anti-globalization movements and old-Marxist perspectives. Their decision-making power starts to become visible, traceable, and verifiable – though not as they imagined. It is a power that changes its very nature by adopting indirectly constructed modes, while still managing to disavow critical theories of the past decade: liquid modernity, happy degrowth, and the invasion of non-places. Even if other problems arise – such as the possible dependence on omnipresent digital platforms – it is not an exclusive, oriented, hierarchic power but a dimension more similar to the potential – in Italy often hesitant – to affect reality. So we dedicate this premise to a synthetic reflection on three concepts that in our hypothesis should be de-constructed: the dissolution of ties in the liquid society,[1] the therapy of happy degrowth,[2] and the invasion of non-places[3].

---

[1] See the work of Zygmunt Bauman where he transformed modern liquidity into true sociological success, including *Liquid Modernity*, Polity Press, Cambridge, 2000; *Liquid Love: On the Frailty of Human Bonds*, Polity Press Cambridge, 2003; *Liquid Life*, Polity Press, Cambridge, 2005.

[2] See the work of Serge Latouche, including *Le Pari de la décroissance*, Paris, Fayard, 2006 and *Petit traité de la décroissance sereine*, Fayard, Paris, 2007.

[3] See the work of Marc Augè, including *Non-Lieux, introduction à une anthropologie de la surmodernité*, Le Seuil, Paris, 1992.

Human warmth creates a liquid society, which means more freedom.

There is no doubt that the future is liquid. This renders the concepts of potential and emergency of upmost importance: within this premise we will see under which terms. The liquid society implies the heat of liquefaction, directly proportional to the rate of freedom present in the social system. If Italian society was more liquid, we might be able to dissolve the "solid" encrustations that characterize the mafia and clientelism. We primarily talk of a liquefaction of power, as Moisés Naìm brilliantly recounts in his book *The End of Power*.[4] Hierarchies are eroded by the ConsumAuthors, which limit their influence. Their role is to stem the control and influence of those who have always exercised power. The weakening of power in its traditional form is caused by three revolutions. First, the revolution of permanent growth: more states, more protagonists, more influencers, and more controllers. Secondly, the nomadic revolution, supported by mental and physical mobility and the ability to compare views. By moving between different situations and conditions, people are no longer willing to passively accept local traditions with which they have become accustomed to. Lastly, the revolution of mind-set. Even children – as we will see in just a few pages – no longer accept the authority of adults without reflection and discussion, as they have now gained the tools to do so. Critical consciousness prevails, even online where it is often overrated in this regard.

These three revolutions change the cards on the dynamics of the debate – they shape and define expectations. To find the solution to the problem we have to understand the source of liquefaction, namely human warmth, which some have named *human touch*. This book will discuss human warmth at length; its understanding and intergenerational influences. It is on this basis that the revolution of generational nuclei is founded. Warmth, as we see in our everyday experience, always flows from hot to cold items. A cold spoon in a hot cup of tea becomes hot, as Carlo Rovelli explains in the sixth lesson of his unexpected bestseller *Sette brevi lezioni di fisica*.[5] Human warmth – a particular delineation of physical warmth – is difficult to stimulate in a fearful and distrustful society. But, when it manages to overcome these barriers, it becomes powerful and contagious. Physical

---

[4] Moisés Naìm, *The End of Power: From Boardrooms to Battlefields and Churches to States, Why Being in Charge Isn't What It Used to Be,* Basic Books, New York, 2013.
[5] Carlo Rovelli, *Sette brevi lezioni di fisica*, Adelphi, Milan, 2014.

warmth implies movement and dynamism. In the laws of thermodynamics it is the movement of atoms that produce heat; it is the movement of individuals who manage their *Emergenza*,[6] as Maurizio Ferraris explains in his short book of the same title. Also, for this reason, the hot and the cold are related with the past and the future, as Levi Strauss[7] sensed when he introduced into cultural anthropology the concept of cold society (those that are primitive and slow to change) and hot societies (those that are modern where traditions are dismantled or reshaped).

As Rovelli explains: "In all the cases in which heat is not exchanged, we see that the future behaves exactly as the past. As soon as there is heat, the future is different from the past. The difference between past and future exists only when there is heat."[8] This is the main theme of our liquid society. It has dissolved due to a particularly high degree of heat due to the increasingly frantic movement of individuals who are gradually disengaging from traditional and cold dynamics, and are embracing a new freedom of aims and behaviours. Uncoupling from the coldness of authority follows generational logics that this book will outline.

We should understand that this is not a bad thing. Inevitably it involves risks that we must accept, but it allows us to live an extraordinary state of freedom that involves increasing responsibility, opening the door to absolutely vital experiences: reshaping and reviving the concept of human warmth and taking upon itself all the risks involved. Here the ethical premise that fights social liquidity at the heart of Zygmunt Baumann's critical view falls down. Much of the analysis of the Polish sociologist is correct, but the theoretical assumption that identifies social liquidity as a problem is deeply misleading. Just as with happy degrowth, a controversial therapy for a correct diagnosis: the model of growth pursued so far is not sustainable.

Changing the perspective, Happy Growth is possible

Instead of taking refuge in the welcoming folds of degrowth, the vital challenge of imagining the future and managing the warmth of human

---

[6] Maurizio Ferraris, *Emergenza*, Einaudi, Turin, 2016.
[7] See the work of the father of anthropology, Claude Levi Strauss, in particular *Anthropologie structurale*, Plon, Paris, 1958.
[8] Rovelli, *op. cit.*

relations, implies the courage to face the themes of generativity, magnetism, and circularity, rather than investigating the intuitions of "crescita felice"[9]. A new path of social reflection, that took shape with the Festival della Crescita launched in Milan in October 2015 and touring Italy in 2016 with editions in Rome, Bologna, Turin, Lucca, Syracuse, Civitanova Marche, Florence, Bari, Venice and Brescia arriving back to Milan for the release of this book, dedicated to people, the protagonists of the coming revolution. A revolution is already in place, one that sees a looming post-capitalist society[10] driven forward by the younger generational nuclei. The last to understand the changing dynamics are likely to be anti-capitalist, "degrowth," and "non-place" supporters.

We can restart, therefore, from a generative dimension: human warmth cannot be imposed or prescribed, but only generated through the growing dynamic of relationships. Online and offline: social networks, like them or not, generate relational heat, exponentially increasing the number of contacts and exchanges with our friends and digital followers. But very often these correspond to people that we know, appreciate and listen to in the real world.

In this new world the most important professions are those that involve a particularly pronounced relational dynamism, both in the interpersonal sphere of care and education, as well as in the digital sphere that emerges from social networks. In the moment in which the relational importance of our being social animals becomes clearer, the need (and opportunity) emerges to develop talents and skills in services for people, not only functional but increasingly intellectual and emotional. In this sense two emblematic examples are the often ignored: the worlds of carers and kindergarden teachers, both are to be observed carefully, as well as all professions related to health and therapeutic care. This will also include an increasing number of courses designed to help teach adults the craft of parenting. For this reason each of the 16 generational nuclei that we will explore, will also contain an indication of "profession," alongside new professions and activities that the particular generational category could perform.[11]

---

[9] Francesco Morace, *Crescita Felice*, Egea, Milan, 2015.

[10] In this regard see Paul Mason, *Postcapitalism: A Guide to our Future*, Allen Lane, London, 2015.

[11] For contributions relating to new professions, I would especially like to thank the magazine *Millionaire*, which, since 2014, has featured my column on the subject.

The digitization and automation of many industrial production activities leads to an inversion in the balance of power between advanced industry and services that will inevitably become the driving force for future work. *Humanities for Change*[12] represents the challenge that awaits us all, both in its digital version and in the purely analogue and material. The very basis of happy growth and *Homo Pluralis*,[13] that Luca de Biase thoughtfully describes in his book of the same title, is light years away from *One Dimensional Man*[14] by Herbert Marcuse, which has been much debated over the last 50 years.

On other occasions we have often explained how human activity is governed by a very special moral focus: the desire to do a job well. Taking care of things as a prelude to taking care of people. Both activities are care work in the broadest sense because they are founded on explicit moral principles in interpersonal relationships, in comparison to products we have become accustomed to through consumption practices. Creating value, can then, have a lot to do with the art of conversation, through the patient building of human relations. Happy growth can pass through these human dimensions without the demonization of goods and material well-being, and, if strengthened, keep wars and fanaticism at bay. As we will explain in the conclusion, this conveys a sense of recognition and gratitude to the crucial role of our structures of relationships. To learn an artisan form of love, care and devotion, exercised with subtle grace, creativity and imagination to the extent that the way in which people become objects of care, and that the objects become subjects of relations, blend imperceptibly in the fullness of life. Recently, at a hospital in Preston – a small town in Lancashire, England – young Italian nurses, who now constitute a recognized community, are particularly appreciated for their work. Here is a prime example of the art of interpersonal relations in a context that is normally marked by the great vulnerability in people. But even the simplest activity of the merchant or the sales person, a forgotten skill is lacking: empathy. The warm relationship looks to the future because it gathers new energies and generates a new social fabric from which we can hope to restart in these

---

[12] In this regard we mention Jeffrey T. Schnapp, *Digital humanities*, Egea, Milan, 2015 (or. ed. 2014).

[13] Luca de Biase, *Homo Pluralis*, Codice, Genova, 2015.

[14] Herbert Marcuse, *One Dimensional Man: Studies in the Ideology of Advanced Industrial Society*, Beacon Press, Boston, 1964.

difficult times, by focusing on happy growth and driving away the ghosts
of commodification espoused in the apocalyptic vision of the old-Marxists
that should have irrevocably stolen our soul.

The ghost of reification

Let us try to extend this thought to three dimensions that are often regarded as being in contrast: relationships, objects and emotions. Contrary
to popular consensus, objects preserve and possess, welcome and express
emotions that accompany them. Objects are magical: they are talismans
that in many primitive cultures ward off evil; bottles that contain genies;
clothes that shape the age of the wearer and enchant even the sceptics;
furniture that preserves a trace of grandparents and grandchildren. They
exude great power and impact on our emotions. This can be considered
warmth, though not exactly interpersonal: objects become mediators of
relationships, like books or artefacts. What counts is the dynamism in this
triangulation between people-objects-emotions that can be passed easily
to others, creating happy growth. Again, the problem does not lie in the
material goods, or in their power to falsify feelings, but in people's heads.

The generational analysis that we propose includes research on how
each of the 16 generational nuclei is expressed through the material objects
they own and/or use, and about what these things express in the life of everyone. Exploring the role of objects in the relationships we have with others and with ourselves. The first consideration concerns a false perspective
popular in recent decades: the mistake of thinking that our relationship
with objects induces us to be more superficial and materialistic, reducing
the time and energy we dedicate to relationships and people. The strength
of Marxist ideology that invented the misleading concept of commodification (another thing and far more serious is the theory of alienation in
the workplace) has alienated us from a millennial truth, known by the tal-
ismanic cultures of our forefathers: that objects are extraordinary bearers
of memory, relationships, inspiration and magic. The emotional proximity
of objects amplifies our profound relationship with others, with life's experiences and contexts, allowing us to cherish happy, shared moments.
The happy resonance of objects accompanies happy memories with loved
ones, children, friends and partners. The problem is not replacing people

with objects, but placing them side-by-side. This does not depend on the objects; it depends on our mental and personal equilibrium.

And so there emerges a second thesis: the alternative to a traditional community and to the social hierarchies is not the postmodern individual, crushed by its "embarrassing" freedom, that escapes from the bonds, isolated and capable only of weak thoughts. Instead it is a collective of individuals capable of a large number of healthy and positive relationships with both other people and with "objects" – as evidenced by the great tradition of anthropological studies[15] – that often transmit and amplify feelings, emotions and happy memories. Thus creating a warmer, and more fluid, world, but no less rewarding or satisfying.

Personal happiness is often the direct result of the nature and quality of these relationships. Material objects are an integral and inseparable part of all relationships. In this way the central role of material culture for the sociology of relations emerges. Whatever a person does, the order of material things in time and space strengthens basic beliefs about the natural order of the world. Our orientation towards everyday objects is one of the main reasons why we accept certain routines and life expectations as natural and unquestionable. Routines and expectations that increasingly include all generations (beyond our belonging), as in the time of generational conflict, driven by legitimate and often unavoidable ideological clashes, has ended. Today the paradigms[16] of sustainability, conviviality, timeliness, and uniqueness, are the common thread among all the nuclei, often creating positive meetings between grandparents and grandchildren, mothers and children, colleagues and acquaintances of different ages.

We can therefore come to our first conclusion: material culture is important because material objects fashion our lives and our personal and social identity. There is nothing alienating in this dynamic, no reification or commodification. On the contrary, there emerges the magic and richness of mixing social dynamics between objects, people, feelings and emotions, of human and material culture, distributed in a intriguing way through various generations. The relationship with objects in a post-opulent soci-

---

[15] In particular see Daniel Miller, *The Comfort of Things*, Polity Press, Cambridge, 2008.

[16] For more information on the theory of the four paradigms see Francesco Morace, *I paradigmi del futuro*, Nomos Edizioni, Busto Arsizio, 2010; *Che cos'è il futuro*, Mind Edizioni, Milan, 2013; with Barbara Santoro, *Italian factor*, Egea, Milan, 2014.

ety is organized according to personal and family systems that are much richer and more expressed than in the past. Thus they are less homogenized and disengaged from the traditional community, but are also less class based ideological visions. The focus shifts towards the creative diversity of each individual instead of an orderly culture constructed on social hierarchies. Liquidity, in this case, corresponds to freedom, and material well-being to happy growth. Is this more difficult to achieve? Yes, but its vastly more fascinating.

Non-places: an out of place theory

In this new perspective it is necessary to revise some stereotypes of critical thinking that have historically played a significant role in sociological thought, but today are becoming out-dated. Indeed, the responses of social sciences have been problematic: anthropology has often produced a cultural determinism, psychology a family determinism, and economics a liberal determinism. This is the case with Marc Augé's theory of non-places, a critical reading of the early 1990's – the time of burgeoning globalization – in relation to places of consumption and commercial retail which were considered as homogenising and disrespectful of territorial differences. In reality, as the great Italian geographer, Franco Farinelli, explains in his passionate reflection on globalization,[17] the advent of the Internet created the space for modernity to disappear, giving way to places and the difficult task of re-thinking the world as a sphere.

Faced with this daunting task in recent years, people – distributed in different generational nuclei – have proved more intelligent than we could have imagined, continuing to grow freely in life experiences through their relationships with others, along with objects and places, to re-define material culture by passing through shopping malls, airports and stations. In reality, these potential non-places are transforming into experimental places. The great mistake of the post-modern age was to believe that the decline of the Great Tales (revealingly described by Lyotard[18] and many

---

[17] See for example Franco Farinelli, *La crisi della ragione cartografica*, Einaudi, Turin, 2009.

[18] Jean-François Lyotard, *La Condition postmoderne: rapport sur le savoir*, Minuit, Paris, 1979.

others) would lead to a disorderly fragmentation of society. On the contrary, today individuals and families who – almost always without their knowledge – burden themselves with the responsibility of creating an order, produce one that is manufactured by the ideology and traditions of the grassroots. In doing so, they are expressing the revolution of generational nuclei to which this book is dedicated.

Such a moral and aesthetic order remains authentic, even if individuals create it over a number of years, instead of inheriting it as a tradition or custom. Through strengthening various "emergencies," certain traits and styles develop that characterize people as individuals and as networks of relationships. In combination with the diversity of the Internet, it unwittingly reproduces the spherical world, defined in 2001 as "The Hummingbird Strategy."[19] This produces new personal aesthetics and new relations with places and life events.

People who no longer follow cultural and religious traditions still exhibit certain values in their relationships: this is a style that is recognized as "our own," of which people take profound possession. In many cases this style with its repetitions and freedom, provides people with a comfort similar to religions and rites in traditional societies, as Durkheim argues.[20] For the same reason, it can also be a burden, a constraint and a mystery.

Today, individuals have to independently create the principles and economic practices that was once the task of the community. The creative possibilities of tiny social cells or distinct generational nuclei have nothing to envy from the diversity produced by a society traditionally studied by anthropologists. Our increasing resources guarantee us creative autonomy: from this comes the definition of ConsumAuthors.[21] If we mix cultural and family influences, social orders and other ingredients, individual households become similar to micro-societies and able to create a network more or less tied to broader cultural norms. The dimension of specific occasions and moments allows a de-coupling from classic macro-economic and socio-cultural analysis, from which we still adopt the out-dated logics of economic status, and the representation of oneself according to

---

[19] See Francesco Morace, *La strategia del colibrì* [*The Humming-bird Strategy*], Sperling & Kupfer, Milan, 2001.

[20] See Emile Durkheim, *Les Formes* élémentaires *de la vie religieuse*, PUF, Paris, 1912.

[21] From 2014, the author hosts the weekly radio slot *Il ConsumAutore* [*ConsumAuthors*] within the show, *Essere e Avere*, by Maria Luisa Pezzali on Radio24.

the rules of social distinction. In this sense, the rhetoric of non-places and demonization of commercial distribution is obsolete. People decide the time and place of their happy experiences, and no one can deny the validity or accuse them of conformism as they have now surpassed old traditions. Paradoxically, the only conformism that survives are theories that claim to interpret the world through pre-constituted critical schemas.

However, the alternative to conformism is not the isolated individual, crushed by a mass of indigestible goods, but individual ConsumAuthors who strive to create authentic, original, unique and unrepeatable relationships, both in terms of places and people, in search of a maximum intensity. For example, in an emblematic campaign by *Google* society is defined by micro-happy moments: "People all over the world are trying to make the most of every moment." Everyone tries to make the best of every moment of life: is there something wrong with this? Today, society is operating under these dynamics, often reflected by social networks. These relationships can include rituals, routines and habits that can also give much consolation: it comes down to learning to swim in a sea of freedom, especially in consumption. According to the logic of responsibility that Mauro Magatti defined as "deponenza"[22]: neither arrogance nor helplessness and passive acceptance of external diktat. Conscious freedom to be placed into a fabric of constraints, of social norms and behaviours that allow recognition and at the same time critical discussion in *medias res*. It is from this theoretical assumption that a regenerated physiology of generations is born which constitutes the weave of the revolution for an unexpected value that we will present in conclusion: gratitude. The impervious and fascinating navigation of our human condition has in recent years faced and achieved apocalyptic passages and hypotheses that you will find mentioned below as in a menu of dire prophecies, to instead arrive in the midst of a regenerating revolution which will be discussed in the following pages: the revolution of generational nuclei.

---

[22] Mauro Magatti, *Prepotenza, Impotenza, Deponenza*, Marcianum Press, Milan, 2015.

The menu of dire prophecies

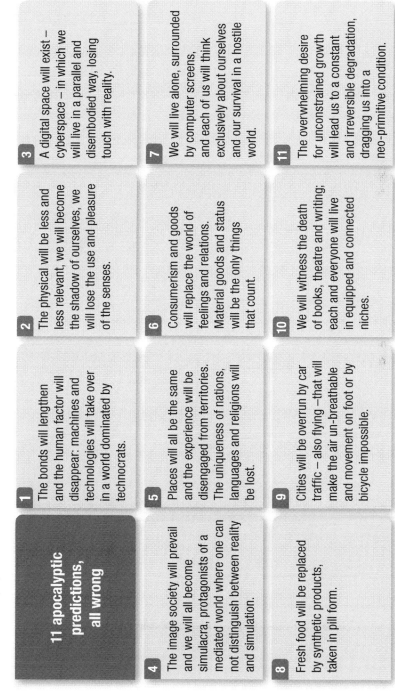

11 apocalyptic predictions, all wrong

1 The bonds will lengthen and the human factor will disappear: machines and technologies will take over in a world dominated by technocrats.

2 The physical will be less and less relevant, we will become the shadow of ourselves, we will lose the use and pleasure of the senses.

3 A digital space will exist — cyberspace — in which we will live in a parallel and disembodied way, losing touch with reality.

4 The image society will prevail and we will all become simulacra, protagonists of a mediated world where one can not distinguish between reality and simulation.

5 Places will all be the same and the experience will be disengaged from territories. The uniqueness of nations, languages and religions will be lost.

6 Consumerism and goods will replace the world of feelings and relations. Material goods and status will be the only things that count.

7 We will live alone, surrounded by computer screens, and each of us will think exclusively about ourselves and our survival in a hostile world.

8 Fresh food will be replaced by synthetic products, taken in pill form.

9 Cities will be overrun by car traffic — also flying —that will make the air un-breathable and movement on foot or by bicycle impossible.

10 We will witness the death of books, theatre and writing; each and everyone will live in equipped and connected niches.

11 The overwhelming desire for unconstrained growth will lead us to a constant and irreversible degradation, dragging us into a neo-primitive condition.

Introduction.
The revolution of generational nuclei

Through the research undertaken by the Future Concept Lab that I co-founded with Linda Gobbi in 1989 – partner in life and work – an on-going analysis of different consumer generations has been conducted, defining their identity, desires, values and behaviours.

The ethnographic research projects, qualitative and quantitative, conducted in 40 cities across 25 countries, have allowed us to collect a wealth of knowledge that, in 2008, was organised into a global analysis defined as Generational Targets and which constitutes one of the Institute's main research programs. Through this approach, it was possible to identify generational nuclei that were able to influence other generations and other family members. This is not "clustered" segmentation according to quantitative variables, but an analysis of future orientation, starting from the new physiology of the generations that in our working hypothesis leads to a submerged revolution, without open war. The revolution is not of armed nuclei, but generational nuclei, complete with an exclamation mark as on the front cover.

To clarify this interpretation, we will outline a few historical references to introduce the 20th century concept of social generation with reference to contemporary sociological and statistical studies. Until then a generation was merely considered as a succession of phases within biological life. Considering the average life span, generations followed one another approximately every thirty years. With the advent of modernity, the concept of generation took shape as a "group of persons, men and women, belonging to different families, whose unity emerges from a specific mentality"[1]

---

[1] Yves Renouard, *Il concetto di generazione nella storia*, *International Congress of Historical Science*, Paris, 1950.

that is formed because of their similar age and limited to a certain period of time. To explain the evolution of humanity, scholars have increasingly made use of the concept of "generation" to understand the context that dynamic forces operate in society. A recent historical example is the study of the "baby boomers" where it has been possible to analyse the transition from the post-war period to the second industrialization, and define the post-modern paradigm.

The author who first formulated the concept of generations in sociology was Karl Mannheim[2]. In demography the concept indicates all those alive in a given period of time. In sociology, thanks to the conceptual vision of Mannheim, a generation of individuals is united not only by their age, but also by the socio-cultural context during their adolescence: a life stage that is the most receptive to social phenomena. As a result, "generational units" of groups of individuals born within a narrow time frame are formed. They become the true bearers of the contemporary content of a particular demographic generation. Thus, generational links emerge that allow us to better identify the common aspects of certain subsets of individuals within generational diversity.

The concept of generation, therefore, influences each individual from a "starting" date: that of his or her birth. But this concept is not exhaustive. The series of events and innovations (far more accelerated in this new millennium) clearly does not affect everyone. Demographers and statisticians have calculated what percentage of the total population is considered the core group in a generation. Such calculations are important for understanding the macro-dynamics. But the micros are more complex. For this, the study of biographies is helpful. Unique opinions are reflected in the small number of "peers": in the description of each generational group we will present case studies and examples, illustrating the main drivers that define and orient them. Macro social phenomena and micro life stories, allow us to identify both a more detailed articulation of the generations, and the lines of demarcation between the generations that, in the contemporary context, are much more complex. Due to the fact that over the last decade we have experienced a true change of epoch, we propose a new spectrum of Generational nuclei. These analyse and interpret the "minorities" within each social generation. It is in reference to these

---

[2] Karl Mannheim, *Das Problem der Generationen*, in *Kölner Vierteljahrshefte für Soziologie 7* (1928), S. 157-185, 309-330.

standard-bearers that new targets were defined for generational "filiation" in the research so far conducted. The analysis of the generational nuclei therefore, proposes new players in society and the market, with which institutions and companies will increasingly have to deal with. They are individuals with increasingly demanding expectations and needs in every field. From fashion, technology and the media, to everyday consumption, travel and leisure.

The generational nuclei are like those in atoms: structural dimensions held together by "strong forces" which attract through their positive charge. In its scientific definition, the nucleus is the dense, central part of an atom, which possesses a positive charge, and attracts and releases a "binding energy." The generational nucleus cannot be so precisely quantified, but its activity can be observed and tested just as the atomic nuclei. The generational nuclei are identified through ethno-anthropological observation and produce an enormous amount of attractive energy towards others, both of their own generation and others. Each nucleus contains all of a generation's positive charge, just like the atomic nucleus. The generational nucleus thus releases a power that shapes values and future behaviours. To study generational nuclei means to define a concept of dynamic segmentation, extending the brand's areas of attractiveness through the "bonding forces" of the nuclei. It therefore becomes possible to use the generational nucleus as the core target: not as a cage or a military target, but rather as a step towards other generations. In this new perspective, it becomes crucial to understand the relationships between generations and to identify intergenerational links, starting from the nuclei. Entrepreneurs and managers will be able to assess the opportunities for convergence between sectors, using generational nuclei to facilitate new partnerships. Companies and universities may also adapt the generational nuclei to different countries, and evaluate the specific differences in global terms, perhaps using specific countries as experimental laboratories for testing generational nuclei. There are 16 generational nuclei proposed in this book, covering all generations and, in some cases, overlapping in terms of age. The logic is not exclusively that of segmentation, but also that of strange attractors.

In this book each nucleus is described through:

- a story that explores its origins, values and behaviours
- a hypothesis of potential future profession(s), complete with a specific case study

- four iconic examples of companies or activities that express these characteristics
- several drivers that in terms of consumption, communication and retail, act as a guide to knowledge
- a number of strategic guidelines in terms of creativity and design.

The Performance Age

The analysis presented here is thus dedicated to the generational nuclei that gather around certain experiences, both decisive and relevant, which mark their character. It starts with the profound changes that new technologies have helped create, along with different perceptions in different markets, and in different sectors. In fact, demographic dynamics and the age of consumers worldwide, when analysed according to a precise geometric progression, threaten to upset both society and the financial markets in the near future. In this regard, many theoretical and marketing contributions are coming from the USA through the growing wave of Big Data, even if some major demographic phenomena are present in Italy (the aging population, the cohabitation of grown children and parents under the same roof, the lowest birth rate in the world). For example, ten years ago in the United States, great importance was given to the vision of Ken Dychtwald the author of the book, *Age Power*[3], dedicated to redefining the pension age. For the first time, America proposed a multi-generational hypothesis of society and no longer segmented according to generational marketing. The baby-boomers became seniors citizens and proposed a completely new concept of old age, in which they studied, started business or pursued an adventurous lifestyle (traveling six months a year). In this way, the seniors are much closer to the behaviours and values of their children and grandchildren. We'll return to this topic in part four of the book, presenting them in the section dedicated to the long-lived – Boomers and super-adults – the two targets of Pleasure Growers and Job Players.

This working hypothesis has been embraced over the last decade by many theorists. The first, *Ageless Marketing*[4], by David B. Wolfe, argues that the values which shape a new relational society has shocked marketing plans

---

[3] Ken Dychtwald, *Age power*, Tarcher Putnam, New York, 2000.
[4] David B. Wolfe, *Ageless Marketing*, Kaplan Publishing, New York, 2003.

based on segmentation. Particularly enlightening is his discussion on the aging baby-boomers who rediscover their civil values, mediated by their experience and maturity. In this way the traditional phases of life – education/work/leisure – are undermined and replaced with a layered model in which the three cycles follow one another and overlap at different ages (why stop studying at 25? Why not gain work experience at 16?). It repeats itself as if it were part of a multi-layered cake, changing the mechanisms of motivation and personal happiness according to the principles of alternance and not complete change. In the USA – and now also in Italy – for example, many retirees are committed to creating new businesses.

The title we have chosen for this passage – The Performance Age – stresses the importance of age as a performative element to consider in new ways, but also a concept of performance which is not limited to its economic connotation, but embraces its artistic sense, linked to intuition, talent and creative improvisation based on the expertise that each and everyone can achieve at a different age, so transforming into ConsumAuthors. They are authors of their own lives, redesigning people power. It is from this perspective that creators of new aesthetics acquire great importance. Depending on their age and location, they can become drivers of the global economy and an intergenerational society. In the coming years, Italian adolescents, Japanese teenagers, young Chinese, Thai girls, women in South America, or Americans in their sixties, will be able to produce styles, languages and aesthetics that become reference points for governments and companies. The generational groups we will present in this book are, therefore, not simply market targets but architects of a regenerated global society founded on human diversity in the search of new forms of coexistence.

ConsumAuthors and new models of thought

Based on these reflections, we will try to close the circle between creativity, talent, technology and new consumption models. The prediction that the new economy will revolutionize our essential values and the relationship with oneself in a single direction, transforming us into isolated information terminals, while imposing the superficiality of existence, and encouraging territorialisation and indifference towards places, has proved almost completely wrong. Starting in the mid 1990's, strong countertendencies manifested, rediscovering and reassessing memory, origins, roots, territory, narratives, as well as sharing and expressive experimentation. This is true for people in both their private and public lives, in the search for new meaning. In the workplace, only now are doubts and misgivings beginning to emerge towards the performative and accelerated model imposed in the 1990's as the new standard of professionalism.

However, new technologies have helped to change "mental" behaviours (since 1995 we define them as mindstyles) that has been universally absorbed as new parameters of thought, decision making and evaluating. The ability and the typical passion of the "creative cut and paste," the interactive speed of WhatsApp, the concept of file sharing, the narrative depth of multiplayer gaming, personalized exploration made possible by geolocation, heightened selective memory through digital devices, forms of convivial do-it-yourself typical of digital video-photography (from Instagram to Pinterest) or the expressive experimentation of Video Jockys, to the sharing of social networks capable of measuring personal recognition through Likes and Followers, have pointed out the way forward, starting from the reality of life practices and the proposed strength of new thought patterns. These patterns suggest a shift towards people power and the central role of ConsumAuthors, with all the risks and limitations that any revolution entails.

This occurs with particular clarity in the experience of the younger generations that are exposed to digital content and become digitally literate from a young age. In the corporate world people often have to abandon their increasingly sophisticated strategies of knowledge management that they learned through daily life, in favour of schemes and hierarchical, functional and defensive models, that still characterize the majority of companies in most sectors. Thus squandering an intelligent social heritage which could in turn lead many companies to make that long-awaited breakthrough: the social conquest of the business. On paper this is a paradoxical innovation; it is only occurs in training courses and often creates a sense of frustration and disillusionment in managers seeking excellence. The answer, then, is to start from simple, concrete, everyday practices that follow the same logic and seem to guide the consumer today: "combinatorial consumption" as the ability to creatively shuffle the cards and information; "immediate fascination" as the courage to leave room for intuition; the "project partnership" as a recognition of the value of others and their ideas, and the availability of sharing and co-creation supported by collaborative protocols; "narrative nutrition," the need to rediscover ones own stories, of people and companies who can make their mark; "tailored territory," the ability to listen and for targeted relations, to meet ambitious targets; "memory and self respect" as reflexive vocation, to re-discover ones own unique paths; "oneself to ourselves" and "ourselves to oneself" as the discovery of reciprocity and the extraordinary power of mutual aid: and finally "expressive experimentation" as a challenge to develop one's own talents, creativity and original point of view even if it means to not always be understood and appreciated It is a set of values and behaviours which involve a great deal of rationality and choice, with an ability to choose even at the cost of being wrong. The ConsumAuthors have learned the lesson companies tend to avoid, transforming it into a creative enterprise, aware of a power that they have learned to exercise. A power they will exercise in the future, with consequences yet to be evaluated.

The sixteen generational nuclei

The new generational scenario that follows the evolution towards people power focuses on our analysis of 16 nuclei, each representing a group of individuals born within the same date range. Each category is characterized by a strong similarity in the way they think and act in a social context, beyond merely 15-year biological or demographic cycles. Except, for the 4 nuclei in the youngest timeframe who are quite different. Technological innovation and demographic perspectives, alongside decreasing birth rates, are the most influential structural variables. Collective imaginary, micro and macro trends are the variables that enrich the analysis and deepen each individual generational profile. With the young adults the time frame of the 4 nuclei is extended to 20 years – and 30 years for the old adults.

The identified generational nuclei, which cover all stages of life, are:

- The 4 pre-adult nuclei are spread over 15 years, from 5 to 19 years old: Lively Kids (5-8 year olds); TechTweens (9-12 year olds); ExpoTeens (13-15 year olds); ExperTeens (16-19 year olds).
- The 4 young adult nuclei, that we define as post-capitalist, are spread over two decades, from 20 to 40 years old: CreActives (20-25 year olds); ProActives (25-30 year olds); ProFamilies (30-35 year olds); ProTasters (35-40 year olds).

- The 4 mature adult nuclei, that we define as post-ideological, are spread over 3 decades, from 40 to 70 years old: New Normals (40-50 year olds); Singular Women (40-60 year olds); Mind Builders (50-60 year olds); Premium Seekers (50-70 year olds).

Finally, the 4 long-lived nuclei that we define as super adults, from 65 years old and above: Job Players (65-75 year olds); Pleasure Growers (65-80 year olds); Family Activists (65-80 year olds); Health Challengers (75-90 year olds).

Part One

The pre-adults

The generation Z of digital natives

This first section is dedicated to children and teenagers that follow consecutively over a period of 15 years, between 5 and 19 years of age. This includes four different generational groups that were traditionally regarded as a single generation. The speed of technological paradigms has disrupted the traditional progression of generational evolution. Overall, these are the four clusters attributable to Generation Z, which follows the X and Y generations in simple alphabetical order. They are the first digital natives, with smartphones and tablets available from an early age. They are born into a multi-ethnic and multicultural world. Generation X are the grandchildren of the Baby Boomers, from which they inherit their pragmatism and the attention to personal and professional future, in a context of greater entrepreneurship and material and personal well-being. Within this generational range emerges differences and nuances that we have gathered into four groups: ExperTeens, ExpoTeens, TechTweens and Lively Kids.

The ExperTeens were born with the birth of the Internet (between 1996 and 2000) and alongside the Harry Potter phase of enthusiasm for the "magic" of the New Economy. The ExpoTeens were born in the geopolitical crisis that followed September 11th terrorist attacks, with the Iraq war and its continuing fallout. The TechTweens are the first truly digital citizens, peers of the iPod and Facebook, while the Lively Kids were born in the age of smartphones that has revolutionized the lives of billions. This irresistible international progress that produces an irreversible and irresistible hold over the imagination of younger generations. For the first time millions of children and teenagers share the same experience beyond differences in social class or country. The web is free and available to all, and the devices to navigate the vast sea of information and knowledge offered by it are becoming increasingly common. Smartphones are used even in the poorest African villages, although in a collective and shared way.

The digital world and all its devices provoke in these children the phenomenon that Anglo-Saxons have defined as *adulting*: adolescents live in the world of adult behaviours, without having reached maturity. Technological development allows a cognitive development and an autonomy in learning that has not previously existed, but the emotional and psychological resources remain unchanged. In this way, we create an imbalance in the personalities of children who, for example, desire widespread recognition (often through videos on YouTube) but do not result in a strengthening of the individual personality.

The logics of recognition typical of the age of development (mother, family, peer group, closer community, extended society) are at this stage of personal development inter-twined with premature and unmanageable exposure to digital stimuli. This shapeless mass of media content, leads to an accelerated aging in some creative dimensions as, for example, developed by the ExperTeens.

Lively Kids

«To be lively corresponds to a live experience, direct and in real-time»

4-8 year olds, males and females

The Lively Kids were born in the same period as smartphones were developed, and grew up in the shadow of social networks like Facebook, to which they do not have access but their parents are heavy users. The Lively Kids play an increasingly pivotal role in family relationships; they are no longer passive players, but active in family routines and unwittingly immersed in a technological promiscuity. No longer simply recipients of attention and care, but architects of sharing and important in the success of relationships. In time, and also thanks to sharing, the construction of their own real and more adult social world is consolidated. Their parents are still an important reference point, but thanks to brothers and friends, the outside world becomes – for induction – highly attractive.

Their dynamism often corresponds to a weakening of the parental role. In a dimension that Massimo Recalcati describes as a tangential loss of the symbolic difference between generations, with the weakening of adult's fundamental role in the educational process[1]. The expression of an anthropological mutation, is described by Marcel Gauchet in the book, *Il figlio del desiderio*[2], and by Ammaniti in the novel, *Anna*[3] – a story set in a Sicily at the mercy of children, where at 14 years old people die because

---

[1] Massimo Recalcati, *Il complesso di Telemaco*, Feltrinelli, Milan, 2015.
[2] Marcel Gauchet, *Il figlio del desiderio. Una rivoluzione antropologica*, Vita e Pensiero, Milan, 2010 (or. ed. 2010).
[3] Niccolò Ammaniti, *Anna*, Einaudi, Turin, 2015.

of a virus that has no effect on children and adolescents. They are the little Buddhas – as defined by Chinese society since 2000, who – focused on the one-child law, normally male – today try to abolish the law, even with little tangible difference. There was a time when education's mission was to free the individual from his/her childhood. Today, we tend to see childhood as a time when one would like to be eternally loyal, as a kind of pure ideal of ones self, distant from all the cultural and social factors that are likely to corrupt. No other moment in time has ever exulted the importance of the child in family life.

The Lively Kids, between 5 and 8 years of age, have an aspirational approach to consumption compared to children only a few years older than them. In their relationship with the world outside the family, they show a strong attraction to messages, products and consumption contexts, although they cannot escape the influence or control of their parents. At an early age, play and games are important for healthy development. These are also necessary for the affective content that they determine, between parents and children, between educators and students. The first steps towards knowledge and self-awareness of themselves, their body and their preferences, are undoubtedly related to the most advanced technological tools. Imagination and physicality are part of everyday navigation around the world. The discovery of what pleases them, simplified by the range of knowledge and experiences at hand, still requires rules. In the game of growth and discovery a contribution comes from accounts of authentic stories, of the goodness of impactful icons. The Lively Kids animate family life through their hyperactivity. They absorb the stimuli of the digital world like sponges and release them with their freshness and vitality. The intuitive use of digital devices becomes their trademark and the imitation of behavioural patterns develops to levels unthinkable only a few years ago. By adopting the consumption choices of the PoshTweens, which in turn become the TechTweens, their speed of reaction and spontaneous intelligence are combined with the lack of filters typical of childhood, which render them often-unforgiving mirrors of adult difficulties in producing new educational and behavioural models. Their liveliness is inversely proportional to the confusion of their parents who as "budding" mothers and fathers have difficulty in maintaining their roles as educators. The Lively Kids grew up at the time when the power, influence and use of the Internet expanded rapidly, at home and outside, creating a world with broad boundaries.

We are thus faced with a post-crisis situation: post-digital natives, from post-traditional families, are bursting with new "fertile mixes". Analysing childhood as a generational nuclei relevant in determining attitudes and behaviours different from their older siblings has been the focus of a recent study, in the wake of the "preciousness of the only child" and the aptitudes that these manifest. Play, adventure, and heroic narratives are still reference points in identifying this budding generation. Classic fairy tales like Cinderella, or more contemporary versions, such as Violetta. Physical environments, tangibility and discovery through imaginative experiences (its incredible to think that small children still believe in Santa Claus), remain important tools in the development of the Lively Kids identity. Learning is closely linked to a ludic dimension. The filter of sensory knowledge is equally important to amplify the positive effects of learning. Fictional stories (recovering a sense of the story, of recent memory) can extend to ordinary and extraordinary occasions to share, with peer groups, which act like brothers/sisters. Each daily experience must target healthy growth. From diet and fashion, to the vitality of free time, these children are looking for "iconic goodness," like a tasty snack, a beautiful courtyard, or a unique T-shirt.

In the lives of children between 4-8 years of age, involvement with parents is essential. They not only transfer specific values and tastes to their children, but also often take the opportunity to create genuine partnerships in terms of consumption. These relationships serve as the connecting element between the protected world of the family and the outside world. In this context, a selection of products play a crucial role in creating a healthy and balanced relationship with the family and facilitate sharing, not only between children, but the group itself. Defined as the "Touch Generation", they grow-up using all kinds of electronic devices and in particular (multi) touch interfaces. These young children become the agents of sharing information, no longer recipients simply of attention and care, but architects and managers in the success of relationships. With time, the construction of their own real social and adult world is consolidated. Parents are still an important reference point (more than friends or siblings) but, thanks to brothers/sisters and friends, the outside world becomes highly attractive.

At around eight years of age, many kids yearn for independent access to a smartphone or social media that represent to them a new world to actively participate in. The creation of stories linked to products or brand

values can be highly successful if they are able to convey simple content
in an original way. Some brands much loved by this target audience, have
been able to build persuasive websites for young children. In addition
to gaining online product updates and playing online, it is possible that
these brands create their ideal product, defining aesthetic aspects and
constructing stories like in video games, where kids can become the protagonists. It becomes possible to identify elements of the adult world being transferred to this generation of lively children, according to logics of
educational and growth suited to them, taking inspiration from creative
workshops within museums dedicated to children and increasingly present in the more advanced urban realities. There thus emerges a plethora
of elements – in the translation of aesthetics, not only conceptual, from
adult to child – that children recognize with great insight and that can
give character to products according to specific details that create curiosity, developing playful codes and creative languages for children who are
increasingly aware of their potential. In this way it makes it possible to
offer a product to families with which children can experiment with their
taste in a simple and schematic way, fuelling their passion for choosing
something unique and sharable, to be exchanged and shared with their
peers as if they were "trading cards."

In term of imaginary, what the Anglo-Saxons define as "Yukky" – a
childhood passion for bad taste, a need to break and playfully transgress
adult rules – is strengthened. At the same time, it becomes possible to
feed the increasing passion (of increasingly urbanized children) for nature. For many children, a cow is the same as a dinosaur, as school nature programs orient themselves in this direction. Furthermore, children
have always tended to play in their own fairy tale world, an independent
microcosm with its own rules and aesthetics. This is a complementary
dynamic to the behaviours of the Lively Kids (who play by imitating the
adult world), and who tend to create an alternative microcosm, where fantasy and imagination produces a perfectly justified parallel reality with its
own logic and languages.

So it becomes vital to invent new worlds before new products, and be
inspired by the structured logic of "stories," that become theme parks,
creating visual merchandising that is simultaneously a stimulus and an
integration of the business, working with creativity on the dimension of
things, the proportions and the play of opposite dimensions, from the in-
finitely small to the excessively large. For example inspired by the fantas-

tical world of literature, but also art, cinema and comics, removing them from the world of globalized brands.

Finally, the Lively Kids are required to articulate the unique worlds invented with imagination and detail, where children move naturally and spontaneously grow fond of products and services designed for them. The success of themed parties for children, or the return of traditions like Halloween are strong signs of the "permanent carnival."

Professional future: Games Masters

The challenges faced by educators of the increasingly connected generations, falls into the category of impossible missions that must be addressed. We have seen how the Lively Kids absorb the stimuli of the digital world like a sponge and relaunch them with their vigorous energy. The intuitive use of digital devices becomes their trademark. This makes it difficult to adapt teaching methods to the standards they expect. This means that it's necessary to revive the profession of the gurus. These educational roles, of paramount importance for the healthy development of new generations and society, must show versatility and cognitive energy in order to excite millions of children. We can define them as *education players*: teachers who are able to introduce the logic of *edutainment* into their teaching, stimulating the interests and passions of those learning without losing the role of responsible educators. They must teach traditional subjects like English, music, history and geography, but also digital literacy skills like how to research online and understand content, in order to help children prepare for popular phenomena such as teen-blogging and video-sharing. The world of education must intelligently face the subjects of a silent revolution that passes through pre-adult life. Immediate choices, of relational speed, intuitive intentions that in many cases ask to be accompanied by an adult world mostly absent and not suited to their demands. *Education players* will have to fill this void, acquiring a role somewhere between a teacher for life and a playmate.

Cubetto

Cubetto is a game created by the Italian start-up Primo Toys, which introduces young children (from 4 years old) to the world of programming without the need for a computer. Launched on Kickstarter, it had already raised nearly one million dollars three weeks into the campaign, compared to the original goal of 100,000 dollars. Produced mainly in wood, it is made up of a likeable robot, a console with a set of 16 coloured blocks used to program, a map and an activity book. The goal is to help the robot find its way home using the set of coding blocks, with the result that, while playing, one is also engaged in "coding." While moving the blocks on the console the movement of Cubetto robot is programed to move either forward, right or left. It is a very "tangible" programming language: the blocks are easily distinguishable by touch and can therefore also be used by the blind.

THE EMBLEMATIC CASE STUDIES

Penny the Pirate

Penny the Pirate is a campaign devised by Saatchi & Saatchi Sidney and OMD, the global media agency for OPSM, the largest Australian distributor of eyewear, with more than 400 stores that is now part of Luxottica. After noticing that many vision problems in children are not easily identified, OPSM found a creative, fun and useful solution. 'Penny the Pirate' is a free certified medical device consisting of a book, an app and a kit with which parents can conduct an eye test on their children in three phases, while they read the book together. The story is about a young girl who wants to become the captain of the Mighty Pickle and, during the adventure, has to pass three tests. Parents can then enter the test data online and OPSM sends back the result. If necessary, they can directly book an appointment with an ophthalmologist. The campaign was promoted on TV and in retail outlets, and has been incredibly successful: over 126,000 families have used the device and sales have increased by over 20% since it began.

Kids Livewell

In America, The National Restaurant Association launched the Kids LiveWell program, in collaboration with a group of Healthy Dining expert dieticians, to provide families and children with tasty but healthier eating options when eating out. Launched in July of 2011, the program is enjoying great success and more than 42,000 nationwide restaurants have voluntarily joined, including fast food chains like Burger King and IHOP. In these places one can find a children's menu with dishes that focus on the consumption of fruit, vegetables and whole grains, protein and low-fat dairy, but that also contain reduced amounts of fat, sugar and salt. A free iPhone app is also available that allows users to locate participating restaurants on a map.

Trunki Trunki

Trunki Trunki is a brand of travel accessories designed specifically for the youngest travellers. Produced by the British design company, Magmatic, and designed by Rob Law, the Trunki products (suitcases, bags, beauty cases and travel pillows) use design to merge travel and play together, creating a new experience for children and their parents. Hyper-pop colours and forms as well as cartoon-like animal figures can transform a bag made according to security travel guidelines (the correct size and weight for a plane, CE safety certification, resistant materials, closures that protect the child's fingers) into a fun "means of transport." Trunki is a toy that can carry young traveller's around airports and stations across the world, replacing the bulkier and less fun stroller.

Nordic Elements

Nordic Elements is the name of a Danish home furnishings company. After many years working in the industry, the founder dedicated her time to creating a brand for the design conscious family. The proposals focus on adults and children, with particular attention to the needs of the latter. The design collection for children showcases both careful selection of materials and processes linked to sustainability that are at the heart of traditional Nordic design, in terms of colour and the iconic and creative energy typical of pop. In particular, Happy Cat, by the designers Christine Schwarzer and Anne Birgitte Balle, is an object that is a cross between a piece of furniture and a game: a beanbag with ears that you can sit on, jump on and have fun with.

Lively Kids

Consumption as

- Life moments to share with parents .
- Expressions of identification and imitation (teachers, peers) .
- Gyms to learn and to manage their own desires.

Communication as

- Stimulus to travel with imagination between reality and fiction.
- Opportunities to explore and interact with new technologies.
- Platforms on which to compare and "trade" with parents.

Retail as

- Territory to explore with parents.
- Containers that generate new opportunities for play and storytelling.
- Places for entertainment that can stimulate education and knowledge.

Strategic guidelines

- **Imagine** simple projects, immediate and accessible and able to promote new forms of sharing with the adult world.
- **Provide** through dedicated creative proposals, guides not only reassuring, but also educational.
- **Design** new occasions and places for the interaction with little ones that can help them to learn, play and grow.
- **Confront** oneself with new abilities and talents of a generation that needs certain guidelines and assurances of values.
- **Conquer** attention through unsettling proposals that are at the same time solid and dense with meaning.

TechTweens

"The conquest of a smartphone is in itself
a way to grow up"

9-12 year olds, males and females

The TechTweens are the first truly digital generation – iPod and Facebook peers – which shapes their delicate transition from childhood to adolescence, which for years has been the bridge between their family and autonomy at school with their peer group. This time of life has been dominated by the pervasiveness of all things digital. These difficult to define pre-adolescents (Tweens – between Kids and Teens – seems apt), exchange homework via messenger, organise their free time with groups on WhatsApp, comment on photographs on Instagram and Pinterest, confide with friends on Snapchat and Tumblr, and challenge peers on the other side of the world at video games.

They eclectically manage their new "personal" smartphones, not merely absorbing knowledge like their younger brothers, but re-working content and assisting others in engaging with themes closer to their passions and interests. They begin to produce their own materials, preparing the ground for teen-blogging that becomes the primary phenomenon for their big brothers. They join their first social network at the age of 10/11. What once exposed them in particular to TV and fashion trends today is re-launched through the power of the web and viral videos, prematurely triggering the logic of gregarious complicity.

Girls of this age identify with and become interested in the heroines in sagas that are designed for their older sisters. Such as Katniss, the Joan of Arc of the future, played by Jennifer Lawrence in *Hunger Games*. In this case the TechTweens are attracted to a rebellion against an oppressive adult male-dominated world that stands alongside the romantic and decadent vein of the *Twilight* sagas. Within them various aesthetics and sensibilities co-exist that are shared and discussed with their peers.

In Italy, and elsewhere, the fall in the birth rate over the past 20 years has shaped this new category of pre-adolescents who, no longer children, often find themselves at the centre of an unprecedented emotional and economic investment having absorbed a deeply structured and articulated consumer culture. In this way the group also has the need to belong that is the main source of energy for sharing behaviours and passions with others. In fact, sharing enhances emotional suggestion, even if these pre-adolescents soon start to feel unique and inimitable.

In Italy, statistics on family expenditure show that more is spent on a pre-teen only child than on two teenage children. This social and demographic reality has given rise to several new categories of products and services targeted at this generation, from technology to personal accessories. The sector that has been most developed recently is pre-adolescent fashion, which has included advanced collections often with stylistic references very close to adult world. In recent years, the aesthetics of T-shirts but also of affective and "transitional" products, so important for the TechTweens, frequently combine with the immediate simplicity of two-dimensional graphic language, giving new life to classic aesthetics. In this trend, the aesthetic tradition of the Far East is combined with the classic design of northern Europe, along with the Pop Art and early graphics of the digital age. Boys and girls between 8 and 12 years now have access to a huge variety of products and adult references in order to live their dream of being a "grown-up." The future challenge will be to make this projection into the adult world educational, by proposing behaviours, styles and aesthetics that are not simply an extension of the "fashion victim" logic, but are able to imagine a creative transition of 360 degrees, from the toy to the accessory, from initiatives to projects allows them to share passions and time with adults. For this generation we must move towards the principles of education and growth, taking inspiration from the creative workshops of museums dedicated to children, increasingly present in many cities.

The relationship between celebrities and companies has helped the growing supply of accessible products that is providing many sectors with growth, particularly for this age group. The TechTweens seem to build their own identity through the mediated consumption of social networks working through, for example, images and information relating to fashion products and accessories. Many companies, including those not special-ising in younger generations, are seizing this opportunity and directing important resources – above all in marketing – towards this market. The transition from the world of cartoons to the world of sitcoms and TV fic-tion reveals the need for the TechTweens to live their own lives, inde-pendent from the adult world but close to the daily vicissitudes of life as a child – albeit always inter-twined with an imagination typical of child-hood. In all these series, the creation of both aesthetic and psychology of the characters is well constructed at the limit of the stereotypical teenager. There is, for example, always "the creative," the "fashion victim," and "the nerd." This ensures viewers identify with one of the characters for re-as-surance in a fictional yet stable and safe world. The episodes are extremely uniform, almost consistent with the style of two-dimensional, traditional cartoons. These characteristics are also present in music and cinema to target the TechTweens audience, just as a virtual fantasy world that pro-vides new generations with the adrenaline boost that they feel the need. In conclusion, for this age group, technology is a right of passage, which marks a new personal autonomy of aesthetic and thought. Initially, only experienced on the wave of enthusiasm for a new, exciting medium that is individually "owned," choosing aesthetics and interactive paths, tech-nological users quickly becomes a way to access content and new worlds in which to actively participate and on which to build games and path-ways of knowledge. The relationship with the Internet for these subjects is well-defined container of different worlds, often selected by parents, but related to relevant themes on TV, in sports and at school. Increasingly, the Internet becomes a world to explore independently through Facebook and other social networks, and a place to deepen knowledge, meet friends and experiment within known locations.

Professional future: Amplifiers of freedom and pleasure

Despite their young age, the TechTweens are key actors in digital re-gen-eration through which two distinctive dimensions emerge: music and play. "Energetic" experiences allow for activities not only of entertainment and escapism, as we have thought for decades, but also the construction of hap-py and relevant expertise and projects. The musical world is moving decisively towards new professions related to digital technology. These professions mix with the great on-going success of television formats like *X Factor*, with the relevance of iTunes and Spotify as platforms for listening, exchange and sales, and also with the importance of music as an amplifier of freedom and pleasure.

Even in everyday life, listening to music amplifies happy experiences, through *wearable's* and the new super headphones, which for the Tech-Tweens (and others) have become essential accessories. Similarly, the video games business has now surpassed the cinema industry and offers a multitude of professional activities, from graphic design to screenwriting. The huge success of new virtual technologies place new boundaries on experiences that intensify freedom for adventure and creation. For example, *Oculus Rift* and *Project Morpheus*, the different chapters in the series *Assassin's Creed*, all represent a change of pace in this market that knows no crisis. In this way one becomes the protagonist in a digital scenario, or facilitates the construction of the stories, intercepting the emotional sensitivity of those who experience the immersion, abandoning themselves to a tangible imagination. Gaming is becoming significant feature of the modern world and the TechTweens are its standard bearers.

Spotify

Developed in 2006 and launched in October 2008, Spotify is a music service created in Sweden by Daniel Ek and Martin Lorentzon. It offers on-demand broadcast of music and gives space to independent record labels. Using an archive that has now surpassed tens of millions of songs, music can be heard and downloaded on mobile devices for free or for a fee. Once registered, you can listen for free streaming mode with advertisements, or pay for a premium version, downloading songs to digital devices. The music can be managed directly by the user, by creating personal archives and sharing playlists, or selecting artists and musical genres with songs created exclusively by Spotify.

THE EMBLEMATIC CASE STUDIES

LittleBits

The LittleBits popup store in New York opened its doors to the public a few months ago. The hardware start-up decided to "physically" show its presence for the first time in SoHo. 'LittleBits' is a system of electronic components that can be assembled magnetically, without the need for soldering, wiring or programming. The 200 square meter store, designed by studio *Daily touts les jours* of Montreal, was organized into three sections: a demonstration area, a part for retail sales and a laboratory for inventing. Ayah Bdeir, CEO and founder, stated that the ability to create what you buy is the future. In fact, the space is designed to encourage anyone to try their hand at building electronics projects.

Archimuse

The online universe is considered to be an ideal learning environment for in-depth learning for the TechTweens. Better still if it allows for the development of creative and imaginative side of the experience. Archimuse is a French company teaching lessons in art history devoted to children between the ages of 5 and 11. It tries to create a global experience where the public can live the past. Modules are offered on Vermeer, Renoir and Klimt. The lessons also deepen knowledge of the art's historical context, and the culture of the period, often using music and scenography through which the children can play a key role in the life of the artist studied. For example, exploring the painting of Vermeer, one can take an imaginary journey into the XXVII century of Delft.

Artstick

Artstick is an Italian brand that produces and sells decorative artisan wall stickers. The incredible success of this creative form of home décor has changed the way people are decorating their homes, especially the rooms of their children and teenagers. The difference, of course, lies in the creativity and versatility that this system provides people with. These are simple and accessible decorations that allow young people to create and easily adapt their own space, depending on their mood or tastes. Artstick offers a wide range of wall stickers that can be put on walls, mirrors, cabinets and windows. The main designs range from vintage, skylines, music, nature and a variety of colours, to chalkboards and calendars. They allow for a fun and ironic continuous game of "dressing up" your living space.

Baby Spa

The evolution of the Spa continues. The emerging dtrend is to offer a relaxing and enjoyable spa experience for the whole family, across the various age groups. Younger children are important areas of investment for Resorts and Spa's, many of which have launched the Baby Spa, with treatment packages targeting the youngest children in collaboration with highly qualified staff. The Dolomites Hotel Toder offers a "Princess Lillifee" massage with glitter, the "Sleeping beauty" beauty treatment, or the "Snow White" facial for children aged between 6 and 10 years. Hotel Asterbel also offers an aromatic massage with basalt stones to facilitate mental and physical relaxation. For the younger generations to have similar experiences to adults promotes healthy living through positive identification.

TechTweens

Consumption as

- Constant search for new things to share with peers.
- Expression of independence and free choice (by parents).
- Access to the aspirational and imaginative world of brands.

Communication as

- Elevated, passive and uncritical media fruition.
- Fascination for the narrative and its emotional content.
- Appreciation for the attractiveness of campaigns with powerful and immediate languages.

Retails as

- Landscapes of always new and affordable products, for a continuous stimulation of the offer.
- Activation of forms of intergenerational sharing.
- Real and virtual interaction with technological tools that activate a path of knowledge.

Strategic guidelines

- **Create** cultural bridges to facilitate the delicate transition from childhood to adolescence.
- **Use** digital devices to accompany cognitive growth in the delicate early development.
- **Reason** on the conjunction between individual stimuli and group experiences with peers.
- **Treat** communication campaigns as exemplary behavioural paths.
- **Consider** the Tandem school-home as an opportunity for growth experience.

ExpoTweens

"We expose ourselves to be recognized"

13-15 year olds, males and females

From pre-adolescents we move to the world of adolescents, whom we have defined as ExpoTeens – that is, teenagers with a strong inclination towards exhibition. In this case, the most significant references, historically speaking, come from Japan in the '90s: here teenagers of both sexes have been experimenting with their own aesthetical identities and other identities for twenty years, in a way that is unparalleled in the rest of the world. In those years, the extraordinarily original mix present within Japanese culture between gregarious tension (acknowledging the group is more than the individual) and creative exuberance (drawing from any source, creating combinations that are inconceivable in other countries), made the streets of Tokyo and Osaka some of the richest to photograph for creative people from all over the world. Launching and following new fashions in clothes (from the Ganguro Girls of the 1990s to their more extreme expressions that were immortalized ten years ago by Toscani in a historic Benetton catalogue), or behaving dubiously (from the Hikikomori who live a virtual life locked up in their rooms, to teenagers who sell their own underwear online), has established a model for a whole decade which has influenced other Asian societies– from Korea to China – and found its full expression in the term Jap Pop.

Beyond the Japanese example, and its extreme implications, the ExpoTeens are multiplying all over the world. They are identified as those teenagers who experience their own identity as an "exposition" and create their own personal world around this concept. Parents and life teachers are practically absent from their lives (64% of Japanese fathers spend less than two hours a day with their children, including weekends. This is a trend that is unfortunately becoming more and more widespread even in the Western world). They have been replaced by technology, which they share and experience with their peers. These young people embrace worlds that allow them to express their talent and to emerge within their particular group of reference. Compared to the very young TechTweens, these youngsters personalise aesthetical and behavioral elements, and try to feel increasingly unique and less homologated. In their world, fashion meets art, graphics meets design, and, as we will see in the next chapter, from ExpoTeens – as they grow older – many turn into ExperTeens. Apart from Japan, other countries in which this phenomenon is particularly widespread are the United States, England, and Italy.

ExpoTeens were born in the midst of the crisis that followed the September 11th terrorist attacks and the resulting war in Iraq and unresolved geo-political consequences. This is also why they are teenagers who need to "mark" their territory, to be recognized in a world of adults who are under shock and tend to be self absorbed. They experience their identity as an "exposition" that includes exhibition, exposure to technologies, the use of the peer group codes, experimentation with expressive territories and various languages, with the video world of YouTube at the forefront. They create their identity (including their aesthetical identity) by extensive consumption, which is often frenetic and compulsive, in an original mix between gregarious tension and creative exuberance.

In recent years, teenagers have experienced more and more independence in terms of their consumption choices. Easy access to low-cost products and the use of new media have contributed to shaping a generation that builds its own identity by means of extensive and shared consumption. Free access to networks and to mobile communication have contributed to strengthening the need to combine a strong performative narcissism with a need (which they experience as a right) to express their creative talent. For the ExpoTeens, places, both virtual and real, become a large space offering almost unlimited expressive opportunities. Even ten years ago, Abercrombie&Fitch's 'New Faces' campaign constituted an emblematic and successful project that targeted teenagers' strong desire for protagonism. It was a collection, casting, and communication campaign that not only offered young people contextualized products in specific consumption scenarios, but also gave them the opportunity to become actual models.

Their meeting places coincide with their consumption experiences, and becomes central in their lives, not only to purchase something, but also to share rules, styles, and rituals linked to the "expedition" of their friendship group, in places (real and virtual) that are most suited to experience exploration. The places of sales and collection that work best for this generation are characterized by wide explorative spaces, where they can freely experiment with products and where cultural stimulation is higher, and accompanies simple merchandise. The perspective of young teenagers becomes a target of stimulation for institutions and companies looking for new opportunities to connect with the "mysterious" teen world.

In order to speak to ExpoTeens, one should not only offer contextualized cultural products in specific consumption scenarios, but also give them the opportunity to become protagonists. The relentless global success of social networks like Ask and Tumblr, with Instagram in the frontline, is certainly related to this trend, while these youngsters increasingly give up Facebook because it is too widely used by their parents.

Teenagers feel increasingly like protagonists and are harmonised with stories, worlds, products that are conceived for them. Various advertising campaigns aimed at this generational nucleus also point at the presence of celebrities linked to the world of fashion or show business in order to create a concept in which a single consumer can feel that apparently distant worlds are more reachable and accessible. The democratization of fashion and the sale of design products in low-cost retail chains, contribute to feeding this thirst for original consumption that is accessible and real. The relationship this generation has with consumption, therefore, is often frenetic and compulsive. All over the world (first in the west and then in the east), young girls are displaying a wide range of innovative and surprising behaviours. In particular, there are millions of female teenagers in the United States who are obsessed by consumption, and who feature in books, films, and television series. In the United States, the experience of consumption provides an opportunity for continuous play, which quickly transports these adolescents from childhood into the adult world with "designed naturalness." Indeed, this is apparent in an analysis of the specialized press of the last ten years, from *Teen Vogue* to *Seventeen*, including *Teen People* and *Lucky*, all magazines dedicated entirely to shopping and all loved by teenage girls.

In Italy, ExpoTeens are true consumers of the digital media, which has given rise to thousands of books and research studies. The issue of speed, which WhatsApp has helped to consolidate universally, is a decisive element in the evolution of consumption, and indicates new directions for something that for years had been defined as an "impulse purchase." For ExpoTeens, immediate gratification is directly proportional to an accessible price, which can make a product or a service – usually belonging to the family of the creative – attractive and appealing. The attraction for anything that can distract or surprise them is an increasing phenomenon. Teenagers all over the world put this into practice by means of decontextualization, surreal inspiration, and by distorting reality in a playful way, as well as by proposing endlessly new and unexpected points of view and personally adopting their aesthetical logics.

Future professions. Storytellers

In the future, storytelling will become increasingly essential, because the quality of life will depend more on the quality of relationships and of the capacity to express oneself and tell one's own story, just as ExpoTeens do instinctively. Communicating will once again be an art and not only a simple technique of persuasion: storytellers will become central professional figures with a thousand possibilities. This extends not only to writers or journalists, but storytellers with images and sounds in classrooms or on social networks, in videos or as singer-songwriters. Everything will once again be documented and expressed.

In the future, our identities will be modelled by stories told by others and ourselves because humans are naturally and inescapably communicative beings. The communicative dimension revolves around a need to recognize ourselves in others. But for years communication has been confused with the need to impose new products. Communication, thus, is not just about talking, but should involve talking about oneself, telling one's own story, as Eugenio Borgna explains in his essay appropriately titled, *Parlarsi* (Talking about Oneself)[1]. In this work, Borgna reminds us that communicating is sharing with others whatever their own view, and at the same time being willing to receive from others. Talking to each other is giving to each other; it is never one-directional, but is reciprocal. This is a

---

[1] Eugenio Borgna, *Parlarsi*, Einaudi, Turin, 2015.

possibility for new crafts (editors and writers in all forms), and professions that will measure themselves with the art of storytelling.

Chipotle

In May 2015, the American Tex-Mex restaurant chain Chipotle launched a campaign all about literary narrative. This is the first time in history that a fast food chain has taken editorial responsibility for creating original literary content. The idea for the project came from writer Jonathan Safran Foer. He was a frequent customer at Chipotle and missed having something to read while waiting for his food or during his meal. He contacted Steve Ells, the CEO of Chipotle, with a proposal to inscribe cups and bags with short entertaining and thought-provoking texts. The operation was named Cultivating Thought. The list of contributors contained 20 very prestigious people: Nobel prize winner Toni Morrison, Pulitzer prize winner Sheri Fink, New York Times reporter Michael Lewis, as well as Malcolm Gladwell, Paulo Coelho, Neil Gaiman, and Walter Isaacson. The objects in the restaurant were only the starting point for the reading process, which could later be continued with videos and interviews on www.cultivatingthought.com

THE EMBLEMATIC CASE STUDIES

Heart Guts

For some years, the Californian Heart Guts have been proposing an original mix of childlike drawing, Japanese graphic design and elementary anatomy. In fact, the company produces T-shirts, pins, bags, stickers (and even framed pictures on request) portraying internal organs such as brains, kidneys, stomach and lungs in an original way. There are many sectors of the project and expressive languages that feed on this new creative energy, which are overturning the classic rules and working on concept of wonder and surprise. From technology to cosmetics and from fashion to retail, the experience of the unexpected captures and "lightens" everyday life through small boosts of adrenaline.

Final Fantasy

In December 2015, the creative director of Louis Vuitton, Nicolas Ghesquière, announced on Instagram that one of the testimonials of the new ad campaign would feature Lightning, the main character in the video game saga, *Final Fantasy*. The 14 series of *Final Fantasy* have sold around 100 million copies, becoming the eighth best-selling video game in history. The virtual heroine with pink hair, who is now the star of the Louis Vutton campaign, is the idea of the studio, Square Enix. Ghesquière commented: "Lightning is the perfect avatar for a global, heroic woman and for a world where social networks and communications are now seamlessly woven into our life. She is also the symbol of new pictorial processes."

MasterCard

For the selfie generation, MasterCard could be the best way to pay for goods and services. MasterCard is testing a new technology that allows online shoppers to authorize a transaction with an image of their face, instead of a password. "The world becomes increasingly digital, and this technology will be the next step that will change the consumer experience in digital shopping," explains Ajay Bhalla, President of Enterprise Security Solutions for MasterCard. "It's part of our job to make e-commerce available everywhere, at any time, on any digital device." More than 200 employees of the First Tech Federal Credit Union in the United States have participated in a two-month pilot project in which a fingerprint scan or a selfie is used to authenticate transactions. A similar study is also underway in the Netherlands.

Instagram

Instagram is the emblem of immediate fascination, which is pivotal for the ExpoTeens. It is a free photographic app and, at the same time, a social network, dedicated to sharing photos taken on mobile phones. Its success is such that in 2016 it surpassed 500 million activated accounts. Facebook acquired Instagram back in 2012 for the sum of one billion dollars.

ExpoTeens

Consumption as

- Basis for the construction of identity.
- Real experiences of shared life.
- Modalities for exhibition of oneself and of one's personality.

Communication as

- Standing need, in real and virtual form.
- Information and a sounding board for one's own performance.
- Means to recount and tell one's story.

Retail as

- Space for group experiences and meeting places.
- An attractive place not necessarily linked to the purchase.
- Infinite possibilities of choice, experimentation and product combination.

Strategic guidelines

- **Design** spaces (physical or virtual) that act as containers for group experiences.
- **Propose** products and services that foster choice, combinations and creativity which provide shared enjoyment.
- **Provide** platforms that allow this target to tell their stories, to prove themselves, to express their personality and talents.
- **Tell** the daily life stories of other ExpoTeens as a way to communicate, transmitting values and emotions on which to recognize themselves.
- **Stimulate** and nourish the adult part and the more childlike sides of the adolescent, both from the inner and outer point of view.

ExperTeens

ExperTeens were born alongside the Internet (from 1996 to 2000) and Harry Potter, in a phase of enthusiasm for the magic of the New Economy. They are the oldest of the pre-adults who most clearly define Generation Z as a whole. They embrace logics of competence, knowledge and responsibility, which, in the past, would have developed at a more mature age, and they are more pragmatic and less self-indulgent than those who preceded them. In fact, compared to their elder siblings, who were forced by the recession to move back in with their parents, they have re-evaluated their own expectations. ExperTeens pursue concrete ambitions, aiming, at careers Law and Medicine for instance. During their life they do not attempt to change the system, but work within it and therefore try to plan their future to reach their goals.

Continuous experimentation, stimulated by digital devices that have been present in their lives since their early childhood and combined with a perspective where expectations are reduced (ExperTeens experienced 9/11 when they were 2-3 years old!). This has made them pragmatic, but not as disenchanted or self-indulgent as their elder siblings, who, on the other hand, believed in the fantasy of unbridled consumption and were irretrievably disappointed by it. Alex, the nerdy and conscientious teenager from the sitcom *Modern Family*, epitomises these teenagers in American society. They are determined not to end up like their elder siblings, who were forced by their impulses and the recession to move back in with their parents. Girls are the most equipped in this generation. Some examples include: the 19-year-old feminist Tavi Gevinson, founder of a girls' magazine; 18-year-old New Zealand golf ace Lydia Ko; the Irish teenage girls who discovered a bacteria which, thanks to the acceleration of its culture, marks a turning point in the fight against world famine; swimming champion Katie Ledecky; Chinese activist Joshua Wong. Even among the stars of YouTube – who in the male world emerge around the age of 20, as we will see in the CreActives nucleus – the female world is precocious and based more on creativity than on competence. For example, 17-year-old, Ilaria Sacco, with her artistic name "Ilamakeup02," has a growing entourage who are interested in her specialization: the art of make-up.

All of these subjects are profoundly aware of how difficult existence is today and how important it is to make an effort to work hard everyday: while their elder siblings share, they *act*. Their expertise thus becomes the very base of their individual and social identity. As opposed to older generations, they have experienced the society of the image, with little substance and capability. They are more traditionalist and aware of the risks of the web – from data theft to cyber bullying. They are multi-taskers; they watch TV, use their smartphone and PC at the same time, and their attention shifts quickly: you only have 8 seconds to peak their interest. The growing phenomenon of teen-bloggers combines with Experteen's need for acknowledgement and with their ability to distinguish themselves through an original point of view.

For Experteen's getting high on drugs is no longer trendy, as it is for many Expos. Instead, they choose sobriety. In London, Stockholm, the US and Australia, "sober parties" are becoming progressively more common: these events include the new technologies, music, and creative writing, where you can experiment and have fun in a sociable environment, drinking "mocktails" (drinks prepared by evaporating the alcoholic content) instead of alcohol. Social networks are promoting this new trend that marginalizes those who continue to consume alcohol. The *Mocktail Manual*[1] is a new collection of recipes for those who want to revolutionize their way of drinking on the basis that excess no longer constitutes a successful social model. They don't drink or smoke, they have safe sex, and don't want a car – the driving test is no longer a rite of passage to

---

[1] Fern Green, *The Mocktail Manual*, Hardie Grant Book, Melbourne, 2016.

adult-hood. Instead, they yearn for well-designed or high-end bicycles. In many countries, they are the most crossbred generation ever thanks to migrations that are transforming the western world. They experience a demographic and cultural revolution simultaneously. To them, gay weddings are a legal right sanctioned by the US and by half of Europe; in cinema they are represented by Ray, a transsexual boy starring in the film, *About Ray*. Their form of dress oozes a genderless style.

For this emerging generational nucleus, the relationship between reading and writing is relevant: they are peers of Harry Potter and have absorbed his magical powers of literary expression. They write and publish novels on Wattpad (the online platform that has become a global success, and which, for instance, has created the phenomenon of *After* by Anna Todd[2]) as if they were real-time reviews, typing on the micro-keyboard of a smartphone or a portable PC. They write and post with their fingertips, without having a defined plot; the story unfolds as they think, experience, and receive comments from their peers who intervene, suggest, and become passionate about them. The expertise developed lies in the strong sense of belonging to a community and in the daily dialogue between the authors and readers; there is exchange and sharing through the *worknet*, and not only the *network*. The relationship with the community of reference accompanies their creative expressions, but does not precede them. The main topic in this exchange is the delicate approach to sexual experiences, which are prominent among the stories on Wattpad. Today in the United States, teenage sex is a pertinent topic. Some time ago, Kendra James, the author of fan fiction, wrote an article for *Lenny Letter*, the newsletter by Lena Dunham, in which she claims that teenagers' exploration of their sexuality takes place in the collective writings of Wattpad more than in the traditional channels of school and the family. But, beyond sex, the success of these stories of love reveals this generation's need to delve into great romantic stories; the same generation that is often labelled as being neglectful.

The ExperTeens – especially the girls – seem to respond instinctively to the need for deep dialogue as noted, for example, by the technovigilant sociologist Sherry Turkle in her essay *Reclaiming Conversation*.[3] For characters in the most popular stories (for example *Left Drowning* by Jessica Park

[2] Anna Todd, *After*, Simon & Schuster, New York, 2014.
[3] Sherry Turkle, *Reclaiming conversation*, Penguin, New York, 2015.

or *Something Beautiful* by Jamie McGuire), sex is often at the heart of their self-experimentation. On the Web, a sexually explicit language prevails without the embarrassment and shyness that is typical in face-to-face relationships. The world of parents and teachers seems distant and inadequate in comparison with these digital initiation experiences that teenagers have secretly in their rooms, maybe at night, within the intimacy of their social network. It is an arena in which – at this age – they are often not alone, but in the company of their peers who intervene with comments.

This is also why they would be the ideal targets for the "inverted classrooms" teaching method suggested by the Association Flipnet. This eschews the classroom based lessons followed by home study approach, instead suggesting home experiments supported with videos, texts and links, followed by group exercises in class, with the teacher available to discuss any doubts and to give a final grade.

Future professionals: Cyclers

In small town centres as well as in large cities like Milan and New York, the bicycle is becoming more than a mode of transport, but a system of activities and relationships that has become been dubbed by Experteens as "cycling of life." In the last three years, more bicycles than cars were sold in Italy for the first time in 50 years. Enrolments for driving licence tests have dropped by 40%; cars are no longer desired by the young or seen as a rite of passage to adulthood. This means the shifting of paradigm concerns their material condition, other than their mental one. The status of the object is less important in becoming an adult, while values such as physicality, body energy, the use of a simple devices, like the bike, which are sustainable and considered cool, are being rediscovered. Bike shops have today replaced fashion boutiques even in big cities like Milan. With the use of the bicycle, ExperTeens, and all other citizens, are gradually re-claiming possession of their territory and the human dimension that seemed destined to fail. Bars and meeting places dedicated to the bicycle are multiplying all over Europe and the US – this marks a change of mentality that will employ thousands of people.

Projects related to the use of the bicycle and to municipal cycling services in Milan have been unexpectedly successful and have created a significant challenge for the near future: the need to make the public transportation service converge with the private needs of citizens in terms of mobility and quality of life. A smart city is not only one of digital technology and a widespread network, but also one that intelligently regenerates urban life, starting from teenagers who no longer want to own cars.

Lumen and GiBike

Lumen, designed by the Mission Bicycle Company in San Francisco, glows in the dark. The frame, forks, and rims of the bike are treated with a reflective coating, a special paint developed by Halo Coatings. It is a patented powder coating, which transforms the city bike from a grey colour during the day, into a shiny phosphorescent white when light hits its surface at night. GiBike is a prototype of a light and foldable bicycle, launched on Kickstarter in 2015. Its particular feature is that it can be connected to smartphones for GPS and has a USB port. This way it can give you directions, connect to social networks, and charge your phone.

THE EMBLEMATIC CASE STUDIES

My dilemma is you[4]

My dilemma is you is a novel written by Chiperi Cristina – a 17 year old, born in Moldova and of Paduan adoption – was published by Fanucci, an independent publishing house that is attentive to what the Internet produces. In just two weeks the paperback version sold 30,000 copies, climbing the Italian fiction charts. The book was conceived, developed and written online using the author's smartphone, and uploaded in micro-episodes on a daily basis to Wattpad, the online self-publishing platform, where the writer does not receive money but can build an audience of very loyal readers. The story is set in Miami because, as the author declares, "I searched on Google, it is a city that I like, I thought it was a nice place for Cris's story." Cris is the main protagonist of the 118 episodes of the first three teen novels posted on Wattpad that have attracted 10 million views. The narrative is a web of adolescent love, betrayed friendships, soft-sex moments and a mystery, with appropriate background music occasionally recommended by Cristina.

The Fashion School

The Fashion School is the first TV show created by the new department of the famous JWT Entertainment agency, which adapts advertising to the future of media, and in particular, to web-TV convergence. This is a reality TV show, with four one-hour episodes on Sky One, centred on the ambitions and dreams of 12 students from *Istituto Marangoni*, a pre-

---

[4] Cristina Chiperi, *My dilemma is you*, Fanucci/Leggereditore, 3 vols., 2015-2016.

stigious fashion and design school in Milan. The docu-talent format, with the creation of ad-hoc branded content, allows the viewer to enter into direct contact with the schools talent, much more than a 30 second advertisement or simple sponsorship. The school tells the secrets of the design profession through the actual experiences of students and their teachers. At the end of the course of study, participants compete against one another in a fashion show, from which the winner is decided.

Kiko Make Up

Kiko Make Up, based in Milan is an international cosmetics brand founded in 1997 by Gruppo Percassi. The wide range of products has an accessible price point while also focusing on quality, safety and efficacy. "Be what you want" summarizes their concept of beauty. Each customer's own identity and range of personalities is considered, and a range of make-up is offered that can be used depending on their mood. More than 300 single-brand sales points have spread throughout Europe following the logic of openness to experimentation, allowing customers the chance to try all the products sold in the retail space. The staff are very friendly and do not panic when a small group of enthusiastic girls want to try all the colours and products before buying. They also trained to provide useful advice to help young consumers in their make-up choices.

Redbubble

Redbubble's mission is clearly described on its website: "Redbubble is quite simply the finest and most diverse creative community and marketplace on the Internet. With artists and designers hailing from every corner of the globe, displaying eye opening talent, skill, passion and enthusiasm for all forms of creativity there really is no better place for you to get your artistic kicks." On this e-commerce site one can buy clothing for men, women and children – including t-shirts, hoodies, iPhone cases, posters, wall art, etc. – from the thousands of creative suggestions updated daily. The website – where you can register as a Buyer, a sellers or as both – was founded in 2006 in Melbourne by Martin Hosking, Paul Vanzella and Peter Styles.

ExperTeens

Consumption as

- The result of a more articulated purchase process, from the initial impulse to the final expenditure, where on and offline coexist.
- Personal choice within a panorama of brands and models shared among peers.
- Showing their ability and capacity to choose smartly.

Communication as

- The diversified use of the social, with different levels of involvement: down to the "communication services" (WhatsApp), elevated to share thoughts and emotions.
- The constant pursuit of things new and inspiration through unofficial channels.
- Dialogue among peers and the lowering of the barriers that divides them from their myths.

Retails as

- Shopping more as a pastime and shared ritual, than personal gratification.
- Micro-retail prevalence, through gathered places and original products.
- The search for intimacy and privacy even in public spaces, where to meet.

Strategic guidelines

- **Capture** interest with products and experiences that require specific skills and knowledge.
- **Convoke** young partners by giving them the responsibility of live and personal experimentation.
- **Design** services and accessories in the direction of lifelong learning.
- **Facilitate** their presence in telling the brand story, transforming them into spontaneous brand ambassadors.
- **Imagine** space and time for sharing in which they can compete using their knowledge.

Part Two

The young adults

The generation Y
of post-capitalist millennials

This second section is dedicated to young adults whom we define as post-capitalist. While they are at an age that is generally exposed to ideologies, this generation of twenty and thirty year olds shows a pragmatic sensibility and orientation towards the concrete goal of self-realization. Their behaviours almost always bypass the logic of capitalism, so making it obsolete: economic capital, means of production, work-value, are for them out-dated concepts, in their existence based on exchange and gratuity, general intelligence, and networks of reticular relations. For them the Internet economy has taken the place of the market economy, with a central role granted to Creative Commons that only ten years ago would have been considered "piracy." For this spontaneous post-capitalist generation – who possibly know nothing of Marx – everyone potentially controls the means of production of intellectual assets. The non-negligible result is that individuals can reach more favourable agreements by interacting with others as "social animals" more than they are able to do as participants in value-based market. Filippo La Porta described post capitalist millennials in his recent book as *busy (Indaffarati)*. He went on "Ours is not an uncultivated age and young people are not apathetic or intellectually lazy. If anything to me, for better or for worse they seem to be busy. Because they are engaged in staying connected, both in solid actions, in exchanging and sharing, in collaborating and purchasing"[1]. They can therefore be *Laid Down (Sdraiati)*[2] as Michele Serra brilliantly explains in his book of the same title, but be busy at the same time.

---

[1] Filippo La Porta, *Indaffarati*, Bompiani, Milan, 2016.
[2] Michele Serra, *Sdraiati*, Feltrinelli, Milan, 2014.

Following these reflections we will present four generational nuclei that are distributed over a time span of 20 years and include a fair distribution of values and behaviours that allow us to define five years as the most appropriate unit of measure for the analysis. They are all Millenials, born in the nineties before the millennium shift, that some have defined as marking new era – Generation Y following on from Generation X, as described and celebrated in Douglas Coupland's book of the same name.[3] The children of Baby Boomers, they have now become part of the work-force, which in 2020 will represent a third of the global. In the United States they are the largest living generation containing approximately 75 million individuals, outnumbering even the Baby Boomers. In Italy – ex-cluding the ProTasters – there are around 11 million. In its 2016 Annual report, Istat has defined them as "the generation of the euro and European citizenship, but also those who are paying more than any other for the consequences of the economic and social crisis."

In reality, there are profound differences within this generational arc that we have split into four nuclei: CreActives (20-25 year olds), ProActives (25-30 year olds), ProFamilies (30-35 year olds) and ProTasters (35-40 year olds).

For the ProTasters nearing the age of 40 still remains symbolic. It is time to develop new values and behaviours shaped by personal tastes, from the passion for travel and consumption, through to an aesthetic sensibility spontaneously oriented towards design thinking, the culture of beauty and high quality that the fashion industry of the 1980's and 1990's – and more recently the food and wine culture – has helped to absorb. Their confi-dence, in others and the world around them, is the result of choices in the context of consumption and lifestyles that still define their identity today.

The slightly younger ProFamilies stand out because of a marked sensi-bility towards their family that raised and nurtured them. They reached maturity during the advent of the new wonders of technology and the Internet, and access to the world of television through reality shows and other popularity contests. For some of the ProFamilies, these reality ce-lebrities represented a dream to emulate (or rebel against), with showing at the centre of their imagination, through strong support from their parents, often one of the first supporters and sponsors of their desires, dreams and

---

[3] Douglas Coupland, *Generation X: Tales for an Accelerated Culture*, St. Martin Press, New York, 1991.

expectations. It is with them that we finally lose the generational conflict, and who live at home with their parents the longest (around 35 years of age) before earning their hard-won autonomy.

With the Pro-Actives we instead enter into a dimension of more adult twenty year olds, brought up in a world of new political and cultural activism with, for example, the 'No Logo' vision of Klein and the Seattle movement against globalization, but, at the same time, in a personal dimension forced to contend with professional challenges and increasingly difficult careers. The consequences of the major economic crisis in 2007 which has changed the traditional logic of the labour market and the market economy, constitutes the personal and collective horizon that characterizes this generational nucleus. They are already better equipped at re-defining the boundaries of their own identity, gaining valuable allies who reside on the Internet.

The CreActives – from where we will begin our journey in the dimension of the Millenials, inverting the order of seniority of the 4 nuclei – already appear consistent with the existential dimensions that characterize the near future: creativity, cosmopolitanism, originality and self-esteem. The re-definition of economic expectations and the refinement of expressive and relational languages for a life lived as a permanent experiment with unexpected possibilities. They are potential knights of the creative chaos with which all their experiences are imbued; they may succeed or fail but they are always on the wave of an existential challenge.

CreActives

"If there is no work then you have to invent it"

(20-25 year olds, males and females)

Taking one step back in digital history, many web experts, analysts and historians consider the period between 1990 and 1995 as a true existential leap caused by changes in digital paradigm, the consequences of which are only now beginning to fully show. This was the phase in which the true divide between old and new economy was built – step-by-step. The Berlin wall had just been dismantled in a painless and unexpected way and some sociologists and economists had decreed the 'End of History.' It was during this magical and unrepeatable time that the CreActives were born. A generational nucleus that still holds within it today the features of the profound evolution of those years. Creative activity and the new independence of production and communication systems, with the decisive shift from broadcasting to narrowcasting, outlines their existential horizon beyond an identity which is too "liquid" to be defined with the schematic logics of classic segmentation. With them, certain mechanisms that lie far outside the market assert themselves: a decentralized action of individuals, operating through protocols of collaborations and volunteering, which generates new forms of economic economy among equals, where money is absent or does not represent the main measurement of value. In this way – according to a logic which is as powerful as it is instinctive, and without revolutionary intentions – the CreActives become the defenders of an implicit and hidden post-capitalism. Perhaps most emblematic examples include Linux in the professional sphere, and Wikipedia, in the field of knowledge; both are representative of that Wiki logic that promotes collaboration without antagonistic intentions, that is, without the ideological anti-system obsession.

CreActives no longer require the emotional support and protection of an adult generation, who are often unprepared for this task and busy with the pre-adults who, in turn, demand acknowledgement. Due to their age, they are also able to explore and experiment with individual responsibility and active collaboration with their peers, or other innovative subjects belonging to other generations. For one decade, they were the soul of the Linker People nucleus, but today the connection no longer defines their character and behaviour. Rather, the latter are determined by their creative attitude, social innovation, and consensus on big universal issues, such as environmental protection and personal creativity giving people dignity. The digitalization of their daily lives is complete, and the real-time recording of their relationships is daily and pervasive: these are the ingredients of the new activism that animates them.

This is why CreActives represent the first true multitasking and multiplayer generation: beyond tribes, subcultures, and monothematic ideological movements. They witnessed and participated in the ascent of the Internet and then the Web: we could define them as the first "www" generation, where the meaning of the acronym becomes *we win worldwide*. In fact, they are the first group of young people to understand, since their early childhood, the importance of languages and trans-culture. This is why they can also be defined as the Erasmus Generation, since the international project of the same name was launched in 1995.

Raised in the middle of the digital revolution, "being connected" in a network of relationships is a fact of life for CreActives, not a choice as it was for their older siblings who use connections to find their way through the professional world (the ProActives with Linkedin) or to meet their family's needs (the ProFamilies with social networks – first, Facebook – used to connect with family or friends). Below are just a few more temporal and symbolic references to understand the CreActives character. In 1995, the first commercial browser, Netscape Navigator, was launched and transformed the Internet into a means of mass communication. In the same year, two electronic engineering students at Stanford University created Yahoo!, the first global search engine, and in July, Amazon sold its first book online, thereby launching the phenomenon – which became mainstream in only a few years – of e-commerce.

CreActives have absorbed all of this and therefore exploit the opportunity of living in the era in which you can see, listen to, and undertake almost everything, whenever they want, where they want, and often for free. If you use it effectively, YouTube can become a possible source of income (albeit contained), and not only a place to showcase your own desire to perform. Apart from Favij, whom we will mention below, there are other YouTubers who, when they become famous, use it in other dimensions. For example: Turin-born Rulof Maffei, famous for his DIY videos, Milan-born Federico Clapi, who went from a career in music to travel video-reporting, Rome-born Luca Denaro – known as *ilvostrocarodexter* in art – or Antony di Francesco, specialized in testing situations of endurance.

Like their followers, these YouTubers experience their own life as an endless creative pool of stimuli to offer and collect. They experiment widely with shared technological behaviour while always keeping a careful eye on the new frontiers of creativity and brilliance embedded in everyday things. A good example of this is Benji&Fede, the pop duo for teenagers, who went straight to the top of the bestselling books list in Italy, with the story of their first album – *20.05* – and its success. It started with the first message exchanged on Facebook at precisely 20.05 by Federico Rossi to Benjamin Mascolo, with the offer of becoming a music duo. There was no talent show, no specifically designed marketing strategy: they used their real names and came through the ranks with the support of the people of the Web. Also the title of their book is emblematic: *Vietato smettere di sognare* (*Do not stop dreaming*)[1]. Precisely this seems to be the vocation of the CreActives.

The moment when knowledge was transformed from prescriptive to explorative and started to define the new courses of web navigation, came the CreActives chance to find a new profession that defines the new coordinates of the future, just like a naval map which needs to be continuously updated or which provides important new starting points, assessments and suggestions. They are not solitary navigators, but experts in providing guidance on digital literacy. To this effect, a new term – together with that of the blogger – emerges that orients the imaginary of the CreActives: the reviewer. In fact, on-line reviews are a highly relevant activity to them:

---

[1] Benji and Fede, *Vietato smettere di sognare*, Rizzoli, Milan, 2016.

from the traditional meaning of "reviewer" (maybe reviewer of drafts in publishing), the term today increasingly refers to the ability to select, review, and tag the most diverse on-line content: from music to videogames, books to YouTube videos. With one click, the young generations can permanently tap on the different ideas of genders and cultures that co-exist around the world, but also on all the memories of the past. This is true for music, cinema, literature, and graphic arts. But not everything can be controlled; having drawn fully from this infinite tank, CreActives show a need for new compasses and orientation systems. Becoming a reviewer can satisfy their talent for telling stories and for critical writing: Favij – the most followed Italian YouTuber with 2 million followers – has been doing so for five years. He gives live talks about the quality of video games and films while he is trying them out. This is a typical emerging impulse, moulded by the nature and dynamics of the Web. It is the same need for learning and acknowledgement of their "teachers," who are no longer unreachable gurus, but digital presences.

CreActives are a generational nucleus open to any combination – even unexpected ones – between virtual opportunities and concrete experiences, to create and relaunch "common codes," without ever identifying with one single dimension. They are the first genderless generation with a high creativity rate, oriented towards expressing their own talent. They are the living example proving that social liquidity can also mean liberty and human potential. In music, for instance, they recognize and mix all genres. Another of their reference points is EDM, that is, electronic music: it is instructive to read through the names in the rankings and the figures reached by people like Martin Gamix, Skrillex, and Avivii to get a more complete idea of this phenomenon.

To them, identity does not matter, and even less does lifestyle. They live in a society of access, of mobile belonging, of unrepeatable occasions. They are children of streaming, understood as a vital flow or current that drags along everything, good and bad. Everything that in any sense is worthwhile and that needs to be intercepted in order not to miss an occasion. They often dream about entrepreneurship because they want to carry out an idea they believe in, and because entrepreneurs are positive social figures who work with passion. Also, they would like to solve old problems in new ways.

But at the same time they look for and attend, for instance, online lessons given by new digital teachers from the slightly older ProActive nucleus, often university graduates who have recently finished school and are focused on team building. For example in Italy, in the Community of EduTube Italia: peppy nerds teach philosophy, physics, or psychology through a web TV format – and have fun doing so. Another dimension of reference for CreActives is the community of Makers, with the 3D printer as a symbolic object of conceptual reference. FabLabs – which grew like mushrooms over Europe in the year 2000 – represent the epitome of this. They organise activities related to manual know-how and IT knowledge, to the pragmatism of "how to do it" which helps to apply the wonders of the Web to everyday experiences, free from any ideological alternative to the world built by previous generations. Their objective is to achieve a credible acknowledgement and a sufficient space for action to change the world without having specifically planned to do so nor hoped to do so in ideological terms. They are not interested in revolution, but seek evolution in human, creative, and relational terms: we could define them as pragmatic and as activists of creativity.

To this nucleus, the aspects of functional as well as creative innovation represent an essential priority in the field of consumption. Although less interested in fashion and style, CreActives are strongly attracted by creative performance, functional originality, and technology applied to everyday life. The most innovative accessories (technologically and stylistically) thus become attractive objects for this nucleus, since, conceptually as well as practically, they offer "new" visions, amplified points of view and a new relationship between the analogue and the digital. It is another example of the fact that this generation is increasingly both omnivorous and selective.

Future professions: Sense Designers

In the challenge of imagining the future and managing the present, we need to start from the creative dimension. CreActives teach us that the artistic and creative spirit cannot be transferred or prescribed, but only created. Designers continue to identify their space in the professional world, but with increasingly specific talents. The world of materials, sound and/ or light environments and their sensorial design, constitutes an essential field of reference in this respect: artistic and creative spirit supported by a strong skill in technical experimentation. Thus, a new profession is born: the sense designer. The challenge for start-ups resides in feeding the creative potential and, at the same time, managing the encounter between *design thinking* and advanced management. All this emerges, for example, in the book *Material Alchemy*[2] by Jenny Lee, which explores the most advanced dynamics of materials in art, design, architecture and fashion. It illustrates excellent cases that innovate by proposing new tools to interpret materials, giving shape to our future living environments, from the kitchen to scientific labs. The direction highlighted by sense design accompanies a dimension of consumption that will be able to grow quantitatively and qualitatively if it proves capable of facing the challenge of the specificity of "matter," not supported by the special effects of communication, but rather by the inherent genius and innovation of the product. In fact, working, manipulating, and designing materials makes it possible to experiment and suggest new, surprising, and sustainable formats to the market: for both the environment and people. Based on these conditions, the area of communication tries to attract the brand and the product, helping them to become "strange attractors," and thereby broadening their horizons beyond the usual target and consolidated strategies. The issue is supporting creative and production processes, creating products and conceiving services, accepting the essential condition of the authentic, original story – always told in the first person.

Kygo

Kyrre Gørvell-Dahll – Kygo in art – is a 24-year old Norwegian man who, in record time, has become an international electronic music star. A DJ, musician, singer-songwriter and record producer, he is famous for his remixes with a tropical house sound, but is now also experiencing great success with his original songs, which are more similar to rock ballads. From the age of 6 to 16, he took piano lessons, which he has publicly thanked his mother for, and then started to experiment on his own. By night in his room in Bergen, he learnt how to remix music on a keyboard and with software by watching YouTube tutorials. His talent then led him to reach 33 million views for the remix of the song "*I see fire*" by Ed Sheeran, and, in 2014, was contacted by the lead singer of Coldplay and by DJ Avicii. Today, Kygo remixes songs of the past and the present and performs them with the original artist, thereby renewing their success, as in the case of the A-ha song "*Take on me*." After a series of sell-out shows in North America and Europe, he signed a contract with Sony Music in 2015 and went on a tour to launch his first studio album, *Cloud Nine*, released on May 13th.

[2] Jenny Lee, *Material Alchemy*, Bis Pub, London, 2015.

THE EMBLEMATIC CASE STUDIES

This book loves you *by PewDiePie*

PewDiePie, aka Felix Kjellberg,[3] is considered the number one YouTuber in the world – 42 million people are subscribed to his YouTube channel. In 2014, he received 7.4 million US dollars from advertising and sponsors. His philosophy comes from the phrase: "Don't be yourself. Be a pizza. Everyone loves pizza:" This is one of the corollaries presented in his first collection of aphorisms, This *Book Loves You*, published in October 2015. Kjellberg, the twenty-five year old Swede has a Venetian girlfriend, Marzia Bisognin[4] (alias Cutie-PieMarzia), who has just written her debut light horror novel in Italian, *La casa dei sogni*, for Newton Compton. In turn, she has become a celebrity dispensing video tips on how to dress and making brief comments about the world.

Decoqlo Club

For some years now, in order to counteract the flattening of taste, without sacrificing accessibility, Japanese youngsters have begun to creatively re-work clothing and accessories purchased in large-scale retail stores. As the most active visitors on the web, they have proposed the term Decoqlo to better define this particular design activity, the happy union between the word decoration and UNIQLO, launching a paradoxical concept, in which the basic and functional Japanese brand, becomes more superfluous and decorative. Decoqlo clubs were born from this spontaneous phenomenon, physical and virtual places where people work and display unique pieces, such as cardigans with elaborate embroidery, shirts with fur cuffs and collars embellished with lace. Often these items are not for sale, but a proud statement of this great desire for uniqueness and personalization.

Off The Grid

Off The Grid is an organization from San Francisco that gives its name to a series of open-air food events where food is served from trucks at various locations around the city. Off The Grid not only offers typical food truck cuisine, but also restaurant standard, organic, gourmet food. On a typical Friday night, Off The Grid has between twenty and thirty trucks located in a parking lot at Fort Mason, Marina District. The food trucks are positioned in a circle, marking out the area for the meal, which consists of a group of plastic chairs positioned on the road in an informal way. This type of event has been renamed the "food truck rodeo." The food served is fresh, innovative but reasonably priced, with influences from all over the world.

---

[3] Felix Kjellberg, 'Pewdiepie', This book loves you, Penguin, New York, 2015.
[4] Marzia Bisognin, 'CutiePieMarzia', La casa dei sogni, Newton Compton, Rome, 2015.

Benetton Face of the City

Benetton launched the Face of the City capsule collection with a campaign celebrating the diversity of female beauty around the world. The models wearing the garments, represented the six chosen cities (Milan, London, Tokyo, New York, Paris and Berlin), and are the result of a special digital processing. Each of them is a mix of different women and embodies the racial diversity of their particular city. In order to achieve this, the demographic composition of the various ethnic groups present in each city was analysed and an algorithm used to highlight each ethnic groups relative weight on the population. Next, the outlines of the specific "face of the city" were re-drawn using the photos taken of a number of models. The result is a face proportionally representing all of the ethnic groups of each city.

CreActives

Consumption as

- Innovative research both formal and functional and cosmopolitan expression of personal originality.
- The creative representation of their own passions and skills.
- Products and services as irresistible and "combined" elements for an always different puzzle of behaviours.

Communication as

- Permanent source of innovation dating back from direct experience.
- Enhancement of cultural expressions that emerge "from the street": containers of stories, narrated on the web.
- Field of application and expansion of their creative and relational skills, often through the web and social networks.

Retail as

- Laboratory of innovation in partnership between the consumer and the brand.
- Convergence and integration between the real and the virtual, according to the logic of true strengthening through the virtual, for example with a service of "technological alerts" or a dedicated apps.
- Surprise and engagement through the effects of gratuity and gifts.

Strategic guidelines

- **Consider** the creativity of the interlocutor as the key to activate a contact with the product.
- **Start** from the project's innovative content to create harmony with the user.
- **Reason** according to unpredictable and lateral logics that can capture the curiosity.
- **Define** communication strategies where reciprocity becomes a key asset.
- **Extend** ones own range of products and services considering the urban landscape as an open air sales point.

ProActives

"Pro-activity helps professional activity"

(25-30 year olds, males and females)

Born between the 1980s and 1990s and still adolescents, the ProActives have experienced the progressive revolution that digital devices have made possible. They are a group that guides the tastes and behaviours of young adults from 25 to 30, and characterized by a strong need to re-process the world and surrounding contexts in a unique and creative way, using technology as an integrated platform. They are permanently in touch with the outside world in order to build a professional career path (hence the prefix Pro) that breaks with the usual schemes of careers aside from the desire for a salary. When hired by a company, for example, they adopt a reciprocal attitude: willing to give a lot, but also with expecting a lot in return. In the past, newly hired employees would ask to be protected and almost led by the hand, today they have a more active attitude. Crisis aside, the most brilliant and prepared candidates (for instance, participants in the Erasmus project, which is celebrating its 30th anniversary) still have good chances of gaining the employment of their choice – no matter if it is a consulting group, a major bank, or a medium-sized manufacturing company. But it is also based on immaterial factors: a not exclusively meritocratic but also a creative and challenging working environment, which can offer excellent training programs.

ProActives face the problems created by the financial crisis in different ways, depending on their country of origin. In Spain they are called *Mileuristas* because their average salary is no higher than one thousand

Euros. In Norway they are defined as "the serious generation," struggling with precarious employment; while in Japan the most common definition is a multi-tasking *nagara-zoku*, that is, "people who do two things at once." To them, the real and the virtual complete each other and become part of one single integrated landscape in which both the technological horizon and the territorial condition contribute to the creation of an infinite pool of stimuli to propose and collect: a pool made of stories, told through everything that emerges on the web and the streets. The story that the ProActives create around their own experience is an extended game of connections, which pre-supposes an increasingly common way of living, intense and full of explorative experiences. Their territory becomes the representation of individual experiences, a visual and emotional story, the metaphor of a uniqueness generated by the symbiosis between the city and those who move through it. The relationship between this generational nucleus and the territory, and with the digital world, is characterised by nomadism: they move with extreme fluidity, from one device to the next, without worrying about its specific nature.

They are, first of all, the children of the new social democracy – new subjects and new multiplayer communities – open to unexpected combinations between media phenomena and personal experiences, in order to create and relaunch common codes. They are young-adults who live (especially but not only) in cities like Paris, Berlin, Copenhagen, Stockholm, and Helsinki. Even in the rest of the world, the core of this generation is spreading like fire.

ProActives are simply not able to be a passive audience: they have an innate need to "pro-act" and to intervene in anything they see and experience. They instinctively de-construct and re-construct everything, following paths that make them feel free in a continuous exercise of creative "cut and paste." This is the second meaning of their name: pro-actives to their core. Technological performance becomes a tool for personal belonging, thanks also to the opportunity of independently selecting music, films, and information in real time. They are the first generation, which from a very young age, shaped their own experience with their friends and based it on the exchange of virtual experiences. Some of them have been able to acquire and prolong their fame in this way. Guglielmo Scilla, who conquered YouTube with the pseudonym Willwoosh, posted videos for seven years, and at 28 arrived on RaiUno as the lead actor in the series *Baciato dal sole*.

Some have defined them as the Google generation, which experiences a mid-term immediacy, often recognizing themselves in a single 2.0 condition, that is, they share everything: their home, holidays, moments of togetherness, their bike and their car. Well-trained in teamwork, they create elastic families with 3-4 people whom they choose in waves. They eat simple and healthy things; rich super-salads, shared one-dish meals, and always seek fresh products. They are highly attracted by nature and, for instance, precision farming, which employs innovative technology including drones and sensors. Living rooms become kitchens and, vice versa, tables become longer. They decree the success of portals like Airbnb and BlaBlaCar, which combine saving, adventure, speed, and on-line stories. In all industries, the consumption behaviours of ProActives reward the independent character of brands and products that can be woven into the fabric of their own vocations and passions. Autonomy and independence are not experienced as abstract principles, but rather as everyday actions that the pragmatic nature of the web has given tangible contents to. The accessibility of products and, above all, services, is a fundamental quality for this generational nucleus, which has made the Web into a means of universal and, possibly free, sharing. The world of start-ups is a symbolic point of reference for many of them, as Alessandro Rimassa states in his book *La Repubblica degli innovatori* (*The Republic of Innovators*)[1], which in a way is dedicated to ProActives after *Generazione mille euro* (*Generation one thousand Euro*)[2], successfully launched by the same author some years earlier. Also the sphere of co-working, co-operative projects on the Web and the sharing economy in general, define the individual and collective professional identity of this generational nucleus.

In consumption (and other areas) ProActives pay particular attention to thought processes that imply a project of relational dynamics that are activated by consumer choices and to the companies' responses. They prefer services to material products and avoid any form of ostentation, even in terms of style. For ProActives, elegance is expression of themselves while avoiding wearing brands simply for status. A similar idea also comes from the continuous use of social media: even emerging markets are beginning to absorb this attitude. In China, statistics show that simple logos are de-

---

[1] Alessandro Rimassa, *La repubblica degli innovatori*, Vallardi, Milan, 2015.
[2] Alessandro Rimassa, Antonio Incorvaia, *Generazione mille Euro*, Rizzoli, Milan, 2006.

clining: now the novelty factor has worn off, Chinese ProActives are also starting to favour content over designer names. In fact, some brands have used this trend as a starting point to reinvent themselves.

In the United States, ProActives are already responsible for purchases worth tens of billions of dollars per year, including an important share spent by their families under their direct influence. The new design frontier that is most in line with the interests of ProActives is developing around the themes of mash-up and creative independence beginning at the grassroots and defining the attractiveness of a project. The relationship of brands with this nucleus is challenging because it is developed as a continuous dialogue between equals, in which those who ignore their own clients are automatically shut out. In fact, ProActives are the generational nucleus that most polarizes the relationship of loyalty to the brand: they can "fall in love" with a brand and literally become its fans and supporters, creating entire communities of enthusiasts, or can take on an attitude of continuous assessment and extreme criticality. With Apple this happened in the golden years between the 1990s and the 2000's, when these young adults where still very young and experienced the revolutions of iPod, iTune, iPad, and finally the iPhone as a positive extension of their freedom of expression and relationships. Music, graphics, photography, data storage and ever more structured stories belong to their pro-active attitude towards the world. The Brand they appreciate most is therefore the co-creative and up-gradable brand, which is able to provide increasingly new features/products and is open to the advice and the needs of its consumers. The allure of innovation strikes ProActives in the heart, and they appreciate the visionary quality of leading brands in the market, above all in industries that are crucial to them, such as technology and transportation. Apple, Google, and Procter&Gamble are the companies they dream of working for, while, among the Italian enterprises, top companies include Ferrari, Eni, Campari, and Pirelli.

An innovation that can be conveyed by a type of aesthetic and communication which is surprising, often ironic, in order to enhance the effect of capturing the attention of these young adults, who are increasingly immersed in the ocean of multi-media stimuli and information. Accessibility is another crucial characteristic for this generational target, not only financial accessibility but also accessibility in terms of use, to possibly include unlimited availability. The value of brand accessibility is particularly interesting in relation to the "nomad urban life" that the ProActives lead.

Future professions: Precision farmers

Farming is increasing in popularity and particularly in the consciousness of the youngest in our society, which the ProActives are an expression of. New trends teach us more about sustainability and production processes, engaging a public that is increasingly interested in the authenticity of products and cultivation processes. The aim is "territorial proximity," to touch these values with our own hands. The world of trade is most influenced by this revolution. First came the Cooperative Purchasing Groups, organized forums that skip the distribution chain and contact farmers directly with consumers to purchase fruit, vegetables, and other products.

Then came the rise in forms of self-production linked to traditions: from homemade conserves to domestic planning. Even in cities, the demand for fresh products and their immediate availability is becoming more and more widespread. This is how collaborative farms and farmer markets were born, which are quite common today in urban centres and guarantee natural products. In this "short chain" of new agriculture, interpersonal skills and trust between people take on a central role: the emotional relationship between seller and purchaser – typical of food markets – is re-enforced, just like word-of-mouth which has been growing strongly in recent years. On social networks that are based on friendship and direct relationships, issues concerning food and its provenance prevail, creating a fertile ground for new professional competencies. This is where the new collaborative farmers will be able to achieve their break through. These are phenomena that are observed by a new generation of students who are enrolling massively in Faculties of Agriculture (+15% in recent years in Italy) to then dedicate themselves to careers in farming, livestock breeding, and agritourism.

Growing Underground

Under the streets of London, where long tunnels once protected the population from bombs during the Second World War, something new is emerging thanks to Growing Underground. The farm owned by Richard Ballad and Steven Dring was founded in 2014, and produces local leafy vegetables at 100 feet under the street level in Clapham, south London. It is a form of sustainable farming because, thanks to the use of hydroponic cultivation and LED lighting with low energy consumption, 70% of the water used can be saved compared to surface farming. Among others, they grow mizuna, cress, Thai basil, radish, pea sprouts, mustard leaves, and red sorrel. The cultivation is a continuous cycle, on racks that are very similar to the shelves of a warehouse. Among the advantages of this underground type of farming, the most important is territorial proximity: the transportation of food, in fact, represents a significant part of its cost, both in financial and environmental terms. The entire supply chain is truly short: it is estimated that the harvest, packaging and delivery takes no more than four hours. The actual space also reveals further advantages: an air-raid shelter has a good microclimate in which the use of pesticides can be avoided. Currently, the products are sold at the Covent Garden market and in many restaurants in London, with the support of Michelin star-rated chef Michel Roux Jr. A blog discusses the evolution of this project and the meetings with the companies and places that promote it. Growing Underground was selected as a case study of excellence for Microsoft's Empowering Us All campaign, on the 2015 World Food Day.

THE EMBLEMATIC CASE STUDIES

Le Petit Journal

The Petit Journal is a French TV program which began in 2011. Due to its growing audience, it was moved to 20:10, ten minutes after the start of the two French flagship news programs – Tfl, the number one private channel, and France2, the main public television station with an average audience age of 53.2 and 59.6 years respectively. The 2015 season of the Petit Journal had an audience of nearly 1.7 million viewers with peaks of more than 2 million, practically half the total audience of the two giant TV stations, that instead fell. Laurent Bon, who with Yann Barthes produces the Petit Journal broadcast on Canal+, has stated: "We are aiming at an audience between 15 and 30 years of age. And mostly professionals who do not exceed that age make the program. We are between traditional television and the new media. We cater to those who are about to abandon television."

Ganiza

The start up Ganiza created by the 25 year old, Francesco Marino a graduate in Business Administration, together with another two young Sicilians, aims to answer the question: "What shall we do today? It does so through a social planning app for small and large groups of friends. Users who download the application can access a list of events close to where they are (evenings, aperitifs, exhibitions) or create private alternatives (movies at home, dinner with friends, a party) and then send the list of ideas to their group of friends via SMS, WhatsApp or Facebook and allow users to rate their favourite, even without having to download Ganiza. The idea is to help young people better organize their social time without wasting too much energy searching for and agreeing to, new ideas, and allows local businesses to more easily sponsor their own events. Ganiza, which was one of five Italian start-ups at a meeting with Tim Cook that took place in January 2016, has over 50,000 users in Italy, the United Kingdom, the United States and Brazil, and aims to have 300,000 by the end of the year.

Natooke

In China, in contrast to almost all other developed countries, electric bikes and scooters and bicycles have lost their central role in everyday mobility with the spread of cars. At the same time, in the larger cities, urban sports like skateboarding, rollerblading and parkour have quickly gained popularity, becoming a symbol for the younger generation of distinction, skill and challenge. Paradoxically, the bicycle (fixed gear) is becoming one of the new urban sports, especially loved by the more financially comfortable that are attentive to new trends. A prime example is the Natooke store in Beijing. Founded in 2009 by a former athlete, it is the first fixed gear bike shop opened in China and a point of reference for this new discipline in its expansion. From an aesthetic point of view, Natooke proposes an energizing mix of colours and designs, all of which can be applied to fixed gear models.

Studio Vacant NL

Studio Vacant NL is a collective of designers, architects, experts in social issues and other professionals, motivated and united by the idea of the temporary use of non-inhabited buildings. There is an abundance of unused architecture in the Netherlands and much of the country is in fact empty. It is for this reason that the activities of Studio Vacant include known associations and institutions. For example, in 2011, the collaboration with Appsterdam – an emerging platform that aims to bring together professionals, developers and designers who work in the App industry – was designed to support and stimulate the potential for innovation in this economic area of creative knowledge. The conversion of buildings, to include ideal conditions to live, work and socialize, made possible by Vacant NL, could turn Amsterdam into the world capital of this young creative community.

ProActives

Consumption as

- Possibilities for customization and unsettling experimentation.
- They seek out modular products, outside the lines.
- Transversal importance of consumer technology.

Communication as

- Integration to the shared experience.
- Stimulating of exchange between the feminine and masculine aesthetic codes.
- Extra-domestic experiences in new consumer "squares."

Retail as

- System of "stations" for urban nomads.
- Permanent multi-channel experiences, oriented to the optimization of time and money.
- Conscious choices of curious exploration (the "taste to explore"):
  The temporary store is conceptually their ideal format

Strategic guidelines

- **Stimulate** specific interests and passions in the direction of learning experiences.
- **Feed** pro-activity and speed of reaction entering into harmony with values.
- **Support** professional ambitions, integrating appropriate services into products.
- **Communicate** ones own uniqueness as part of a rich and complex everyday life.
- **Define** shared meeting spaces, with the aim of exchanging life experiences.

ProFamilies

ProFamilies are young adults who define their social identity with great continuity in comparison to their family. Family is first among the values expressed and declared. Born in the early 1980's, in Italy they are the first children who were subjected to the trauma of separated parents, while simultaneously living the dream of "Reagan style hedonism" within society. Although they are consumption experimenters and innovators, they are far more traditionalist than their parents with regards to affection and the family. Because of the economic crisis that caught them unprepared at the age of 25, they are now 30-35 and still closely connected to their family, often still living at home with their parents (or parent). Thus, they personify the precise opposite of the generational conflict experienced in the '60s and '70s. Often they are only children born into wealthy families, they are immature and "NEET" (Not engaged in Education, Employment or Training): there are multiple definitions for this generation. They represent the warning signs of a generation whose expectations were betrayed and who are now seeking a psychological and financial safety net within their family. In Italy, they suffered the illusions of the Berlusconian videocracy, dreaming about becoming showgirls or male stars on TV shows. They have absorbed the impact of Big Brother and the Taricone syndrome, for ten years sure that appearing on television would be the solution to their identity issues and their professional problems. Today, appearance still is an essential element in their life choices, just like the forms of "identity consumption." They are and feel unique, but they are constantly searching for the siblings they never had. This is a generational nucleus that represents the warm heart of the consumption society, from China to the Mediterranean. In the United States, they directly engage in solving concrete problems for their family. As in the case of Kate Marie Sigfusson, a 30 years old, with a 21-month old son and a second one on the way, who founded Babies4babies, a start-up created in Chicago two years ago to defend the idea of considering both her children and her career important. They are people who are busy earning a living and developing their careers in financial performances that constitute their existential horizon. Teetering between the mythology of capitalism and return to familism, they use the Web to substantiate their central role in the world. Their desire to try everything, and to expand and exasperate the rules imposed by previous generations, represents the core of many events, which are only apparently transgressive. The meaning of success for ProFamilies includes an idea of exclusivity, excess, and exhibition. It is not only about having the best, but also about showing it off and displaying wealth. Social status is still fundamental to them and to their families: this is an element of their profile that marks a discontinuity with respect to the CreActives and ProActives, who are only a few years younger.

The encounter between their values and the need for modernity stimulates the ProFamilies to revisit types of traditional products that are able to support the new dynamics of everyday life. By maintaining the original qualities but adapting them to the more contemporary dimension, new consumption situations and product categories are born. For young male ProFamilies, this is expressed in a passion for tailoring, and is identified in the search for icons of more classic femininity for girls (flowers, butterflies, high heels, details with a romantic inspiration), as well as in a more formal elegance, which is strongly returning to mainstream fashion and is apparent on streets all around the world.

From the point of view of behaviour, this generation of young people works hard to achieve personal success, maybe walking in the footsteps of a family tradition and working in professions inherited from their parents or relatives. While for CreActives and ProActives the web is a form of relationship, with new logics and potential; for ProTasters it is a means for sharing ideas and sensitivity; and for ProFamilies the Web mainly functions as a virtual audience they can perform to using their own uniqueness and, as they get older, it even becomes a source of styles, behaviours and values to share.

Exclusive communities become the virtual counterpart to private clubs that they often attend or at least aspire to following in the tracks of their parents. Technology is often used as a luxury accessory to be displayed, but we should not underestimate their ability to use it to define their own bespoke service. In the field of consumption, what increasingly matters are proposals that can sustain the self-centred nature of ProFamilies, who search for the daily performance of services and products, but are plunged into a context of existential quality and exclusivity, with a strong link to their family.

In this moment of crisis – in the economy and in our values – ProFamilies are clinging on to a close ally: their own group of reference, whether it is family or friends. An objects ability to communicate material qualities and make people's social status concrete makes products and, secondly, services the centre of attention for ProFamilies. Apart from the aesthetical value of objects, their symbolic value also takes on crucial relevance. The latter is an intangible but essential factor to create an ideal world of reference that anyone can recognize: from vintage and family tradition to high quality local craftsmanship. We could talk about a "vanity fair" in which the tangible and intangible are interweaved: products and services that aim at the neo-romantic without forgetting the importance of the self-celebration of the futile. In fact, ProFamilies are more loyal to their brands of reference than the other younger generational nuclei. They trust brands more, and are more passive, thus giving foundation to a generally unilateral communication from the Brand to the consumer. Taylor Swift, the singer, songwriter, and actress who was immortalized on the cover of Vogue Australia and who sings "New Romantic" and "I want to surprise, not to shock," can be considered as their muse. Familiarity, in any case, is a decisive value to them. They look for identification between the uniqueness of the brand and their own uniqueness. For instance, they appreciate the intelligent use of testimonials in communication: like in Chloé's 2016 Resort Collection which re-interprets the musical epic of Roxy Music, or the voice of Alison Moyet for Burberry or Jonathan W. Anderson for the brand Loewe. Or with Riccardo Tisci who entitled his first New York fashion show for Givenchy, *I believe in the power of love*. The Brands they seek are certainly distinctive, with an acknowledged identity, often classic, but with the essential ability to renew themselves: as in the case of

Alessandro Michele for Gucci who created a wardrobe of new tenderness, mixed with the memories of a thoughtful and courteous past. The symbolic dimension that the brand needs to underline in order to meet the preferences of ProFamilies is more iconic, in terms of languages, and at the same time more archetypical in relation to the identity of the brand itself. Knowing how to creatively re-elaborate your own historical personality by updating it, working on the logo, and anchoring the contemporary aesthetics to vintage details and sensitivities are all techniques that attract ProFamilies and awaken their curiosity. The proximity of this generational nucleus to the brand, which comes from their need for self-definition and for identifying themselves in an élite group of individuals, is evolving and "ennobling" itself by means of intellectual re-elaboration, which the consumer is often willing to delegate to the company.

Future professions: Daily Problem Solvers

Often when we think about digital society we imagine an abstract world in which our bodies and senses lose their relevance in favour of a general loss of relational weight. These convictions lead to a certain mistrust in technological innovation and the marvels of the digital world. But when we observe the daily lives of real people – for example, the ProFamilies – we notice that much of this resistance disappears. Grandparents are talking to their grandchildren on Skype, different generation shares happy moments on Instagram, and music fans build their musical memories with Shazam. Some amplify and integrate their own passions, others extend their network of contacts around the world; everyone considers health and physical fitness as a new religion. What prevails over all this is a trend oriented towards specificity: Big Data analysis, in which the Anglo-Saxons are the masters of our day, indicates the relationship between behaviours, problems, and solutions. It opens up an entire dimension that moves through the liquid society, providing indications about the most effective practices that reach statistically significant results. Consultancy opens up towards a new interpersonal dimension, less professional in the purely corporate sense, and more oriented towards each individual, who become privileged customers.

The professional space that opens in this dimension can be defined using the expression *problem solver* (he who solves problems) and is very broad: in companies, marketing managers are becoming *insighters*, careful observers of consumption phenomena who hunt for new solutions in everyday life. In the digital world, young programmers are dedicated to inventing Apps that prove to be valuable in integrating and completing the performance of a product or a brand. In this paradigmatic revolution, a new discipline emerges that feeds new professions: the service designer. In the past, this field of expertise was limited to developing interfaces and graphics, while today they give products new life and regenerate their performance. All this finds a rich and articulated application in the dimension of consultancy services for ProFamilies that go through all spheres of daily life, from food to urban transportation.

Babies4Babies

Kate Marie Sigfusson, a young woman from Chicago, founded her business when she became a mother, and proved how motherhood and children can be a driver in reaching new values and business prospects, instead of being an obstacle to self-realization. Through Babies4babies, Kate Marie sells luxury blankets for children, made in America with high quality materials and an ethical and sustainable supply chain, with the promise that, for every purchase they will finance 4 kits for the antiseptic treatment of new-born babies in developing countries. The website of this small entrepreneurial activity, which has a very sophisticated style, clearly communicates the founder's will to leave a mark in the world of the Millennials who are becoming mothers. Next to the narrative are images focusing on Kate Marie's adventure. There is an entire section dedicated to other "start-up moms" who have been able to combine business and family with satisfaction, style, and a desire to emerge.

THE EMBLEMATIC CASE STUDIES

Urban Garden Collection

Thompson & Morgan, an historical English company specialized in gardening products, has launched (in collaboration with the Royal Botanical Gardens) the Urban Garden Collection, a range of seeds for vegetables that is supposed to undermine the idea that you need a big space to have a vegetable garden. The proposed plant varieties have been selected for growing in pots or in small spaces, allowing everybody to get involved in this type of cultivation. The project responds to a growing demand for vegetable seeds, which have increased sales by 60% in the United Kingdom, a market that is responsive to green fingers, but also to the financial savings that this type of cultivation guarantees. From an aesthetic point of view, the project proves interesting, both for the packaging design and the impact these products will have on urban landscapes.

Electric Objects

Electric Objects is a digital art platform using the internet-connected screen EO1, desi-gned specifically for art and capable of playing video, animations, high definition images, or web-based work. Its mission is to put digital art on a wall in every home, and thereby affording to digital art the same time and space that we give to paintings and photo-graphy. When you join Electric Objects, you're invited to download the Electric Objects apps for iOS and Android. With these apps, you can explore thousands of works of art shared by members of the Electric Objects community, or discover original art made exclusively for Electric Objects in Art Clubs. In December 2015, Electric Objects opened the first incarnation of the Electric Objects Showroom in New York at a space in the heart of Soho, dedicated to showcasing new works from an amazing group of artists, including collections from artists like Björk, Ai Weiwei, Zach Gage, YACHT, Sabrina Ratte, and others. Visitors to the Showroom are also given exclusive access to a limited edition handmade wooden frame for their EO1.

Beautified

This app, conceived by Hannah Bronfman with Annie Evans and Peter Hananel, provides an online platform to reserve a wide range of beauty services, including massages, beau-ty treatments, manicures, pedicures, and makeup. Active in New York, and soon in Chica-go and Los Angeles as well, it offers an extensive list of beauty salons, hairdressers, and spa centres to choose from. The specificity and originality of the app is to offer beauty and wellness services bookable and accessible within 24 hours, starting at 6.00am. It offers itself as a partner that enhances everyday life, offering excellent service guaranteed by carefully selected suppliers. Including, among others, John Barrett Salon, Warren-Trico-mi, Caudalie, Shibui Spa and Tenoverten. The founder, Hannah Bronfman states that: "our new application is like Uber but for all beauty lovers." The future of Beautified is to expand into the world of fitness, thus making it possible to book a Pilates or Spin session in the closest and most convenient gym within an hour.

Woven Playgrounds

For Alexandra Kehayoglou, creating carpets is more a vocation than a choice. The desi-gner, of Greek origin, has weaving in her DNA. In her studio in Buenos Aires, the fabric scraps arrive from the El Espartano factory, a company owned by the Kehayoglou family, which is a real reference point in the world of design. Rather than creating simple carpets, Alexandra collections consist of large textile reliefs created by the technique of tufting. Her compositions take on new and unexpected forms, as in the case of the Pastureland and Garden collections, in which the artist is inspired by textures found in nature like moss, sand, water, bark and green pastures. Dries Van Noten commissioned an impres-sive grassy carpet in wool as a spectacular catwalk for his spring 2015 collection fashion show.

ProFamilies

Consumption as

- A personal narcissistic expression of uniqueness.
- The search for brands with strong family values.
- Access to a world of everyday exclusivity.

Communication as

- A container and provider of styles, behaviours and values.
- Stimulation as an emulative and aspirational behaviour towards the star system
- The charm of classic and retro icons, creatively reworked.

Retail as

- Gateway to a world of excellence; for example, through the concept store format appreciated for the richness and variety of products, services and activities to be explored, even with the family.
- A moment for tangible gratification and "luxurious comfort."
- The access point to a world of excellence, offering "tailored" quality.

Strategic guidelines

- **Produce** and propose style icons, tastes and behaviours, creating new languages, decorations, product categories and fruitions.
- **Create** the conditions to feel at the centre of different proposals and activities, in which to reconcile one's own egocentrism.
- **Activate** the free spirit of youth with a trendsetter sophistication, attributable to their peer group.
- **Deepen** the excellence of made to measure services, with an attention to detail and must have combinations closer to a more formal elegance.
- **Interpret** and model the places of purchase inspired by the creative challenge of being 'unique' in all forms of self-expression.

ProTasters

"I'm oriented towards pleasure and pleasing myself"

(35-40 year olds, males and females)

Born and raised during the great awakening of hedonistic society, after the conflicts and traumas of the 1970's, ProTasters have had the time and ability to metabolize everything that is tasteful: from fashion, design, and the recent glories of enogastronomy. The ProTasters personify the ideal world of the new forty year olds: they are men and above all women who are characterized by a pronounced sensorial refinement and who show their emotions through everyday consumption choices, using original communication codes. These subjects are highly sensitive to the outside world and to what is proposed to them; they show great self-awareness and know what to look for.

For ProTasters, intuition and perception are complex psychological mechanisms, but at the same time they are very concrete, since interior richness moves through the senses. Sensorial reality thus becomes a gateway to an increasingly fascinating internal world, which, for this generational nucleus in particular, has transformed the hedonism of the 1980's into a source of discovering their potential by means of the "little everyday things." Single or in a relationship, they invest a great deal of energy on creating a home environment that is as close as possible to their ideal: the home is a microcosm that reflects their deepest taste.

The world of ProTasters is able to build vital experiences and give interpretations starting from intuitive sensitivity, and they search for new balances and natural harmonies. The products and services they demand need to become instruments to make it easier to define new languages and aesthetic codes. What matters to them are extraordinary care and an artistic touch.

This nucleus produces aesthetics that are very advanced from the sensorial point of view: from the creation of landscapes and conditions in which the visual, auditive and tactile elements meet and create new and magical effects, to the importance of the physical body experienced at 360 degrees, the search for a beauty that is never superficial, but always the expression of harmony between an external and internal world. In particular, the female component of the nucleus experiences the suggestive and deep allure of the original beauty of an object and above all of a place where the sensorial attraction is Nature itself, with its depth and evocative power. Technology and nature thus become two important dimensions (alternative and complementary) lying at the base of this generation's life experiences.

ProTasters tend to fall in love with, or feel a strong fascination for, the products they choose: as post-narcissist subjects, they project part of their personality onto the world of consumption. In relation to their behaviour, rituals take on particular relevance: unusual rites, or rites that didn't exist in the past, are desired and appreciated. New occasions to share everyday experiences in playful or more serious terms are introduced, thus linking the product to the occasion itself with a double thread. By preserving its original features, but adapting them to the more contemporary dimension, create new occasions of use and new product categories.

The search for care starts from the self, and later expresses itself through objects and places of experience: travel is certainly an example of this way of acting. On a trip, ProTasters search for sophisticated and individual microcosms of experience. The use of sophisticated structures and specialized technologies during the journey stimulates forms of emotional experiences within them and allows them to imagine "sensorial" guides. Operators in the tourism and hospitality industry could therefore become the most powerful "amplifiers" of the emotion and culture of the territory in their eyes. In fact, the great new desire they express is giving value to travelling – be it a short weekend trip, an excursion with the family or an exotic trip for pleasure or business – to stimulate their curiosity, follow their passions, and multiply moments of wellbeing and pleasure. Intuition and perception are – in this strategy – decisive passages for a travel experience that in their eyes demands operators who are much closer to the

profession of cultural mediators than simple companions in leisure, entertainment and pleasure.

To ProTasters, more frequent travel takes on the initiatory characteristics of a personal or family workshop, in which their own identity is shaped
as individuals who favour true exploration over easy evasion. In fact, in
travel they demand to be present to themselves. In addition, because their
story is increasingly played though this explorative impulse, it literally ex-
plodes on social networks.

In particular, this generation of forty-year-olds personifies the expression *de gustibus non disputandum est* as Emanuele Arielli brilliant recent
book *Farsi piacere*[1] tells us – where the author, precisely, wants to taste the
journey. They are hunting for vital experiences, in an attempt to give new
meaning and a new interpretation to the places they experience, photograph, tell their friends about; starting from an aesthetic and "literary"
sensitivity in the search of new balances between culture and nature.

Even new spas – wellness centres that offer holistic care for the person,
including food, workouts, saunas, and massage areas – are experienced not
so much as places to practice sports, but more as islands of regeneration in
which to spend a whole day, and which are easily reconciled with a persons
aspirations. From a global geographic perspective, one of the places that
seems to best represent the chosen area of this generation today is South
America, which, with originality and freshness, is appearing on the stage
of global society for the first time. Some basic characteristics distinguish
South American culture: a total interpenetration of perceptive culture, from
music to the taste of fruits, the central role of sensorial experience, the high
artisanal quality of production, the concentrated variety of their aesthetic
expressions, and the centrality of the body. All of these characteristics make
it rather likely that this area will be the aesthetic needle on the scale of the
global scene in the future, which is characterized by the social and economic
superpowers of other emerging countries like China and India. In particular, women (and a class of young women who are emerging in art, culture
and entrepreneurship) are marking the culture of this part of the world,
which is proving to be increasingly in line with the advanced needs of a
market that rewards the meeting of East and West, and which is very close
to the characteristics of the ProTasters as described here.

---

[1] Emanuele Arielli, *Farsi piacere. La costruzione del gusto*, Raffaello Cortina Editore, Milan, 2016.

Refined, sensitive, exotic, ProTasters ultimately propose an aesthetic
that is far removed from television banalities, and use the media as a vehicle to re-enforce their own uniqueness. They place themselves at the
centre of an ethical and aesthetic revolution in which harmony, gestures,
narrative taste and care, mark a deep shift of paradigm, which neutralizes
the a-critical race towards modernization which many Asian nations are
running towards and which is deeply influencing Western countries.

In this case, it will not be the Far East leading this transformation, but
rather Central Asia and the Buddhist and Hindu communities. Together
with Brazil, China, India, a key role will be played by Thailand and Japan,
followed by countries with a great tradition of female freedom and refinement: Denmark, Holland, France.

The system of consumption is increasingly perceived by ProTasters as a
stage they can move on as protagonists, in the search for new user-related
emotions.

Brands, with their products and services, will need to learn to govern
these new emotional balances in order to benefit from them. This generational nucleus avoids the risk of manipulation by constantly seeking
feedback from, and harmony with, the company. In their daily experience, ProTasters pay particular attention to experiences linked to the use
of goods and services, to the places of consumption and to environments
that give an added value to pure purchase. Emotional implications are of
fundamental importance in the choices of this generational nucleus, which
feels the need for a new "sentimental education" through conscious control
of their feelings and emotions, rather than relying on reason or knowledge.
ProTasters' relationship with brands is less critical and interactive compared to that of ProActives, but no less demanding. In fact, they are receptive young adults who are willing to listen, but who nonetheless look for
a deep harmony with the brand, which can therefore be easily neglected.

"Fine tuning" is a need in the relationship between the brand and
ProTasters in order to meet their expectations. Loyalty to the brand is
strengthened when there is empathy; otherwise the relationship remains
rather cold. The brands they appreciate most are therefore empathic
brands, which have a strong aesthetical sensitivity and an artistic vision to
share with their consumers.

A brands selective quality and editorial capacity are highly relevant for
ProTasters, both when they are aimed at the consumer to develop a refined
product personalization, and when they are oriented towards the creation

of an actual "brand home," carefully studied and articulated, that they can visit or even inhabit.

The spaces where services are sold and consumed are actual "strange attractors" and the aesthetical dimension is moving towards the poly-sensorial, to create "partial paradises" in which nature often has an influence on inspiring and enriching the "brand experience." Today, this experience goes increasingly in the direction of an almost magical alchemic ability that matches the favourite ProTasters consumption sector – wellbeing and personal care.

Future professions: Taste dispensers

Today, in Italy and the rest of the world, bars are increasingly at the centre of urban society and are proving to be permanent meeting places for ProTasters, who consider coffee and hot chocolate their favourite products.

This means that, professionally speaking, taste can be considered – even for the new generations – as an extraordinary workshop of opportunities. Chefs and barmen have entered the collective imagination next to fashion designers and product designers, stimulating new horizons for "taste dispensers." Wine, craft beer, chocolate and coffee represent just some of the emblematic examples of this comeback of taste understood in its various forms. In terms of professional opportunities, opening a bar is a possibility for young entrepreneurs and retailers who attempt to create a virtuous triangle between music, informal hospitality and quality coffee. The annual *Gambero Rosso* Guide to bars in Italy assigns a prize to the best bar in Italy and thus points to a possible way of integrating physical and virtual networks in which the outdoor prevails over the indoors. All around the world, bars have today become a place of aggregation in which the surprising combination of different functions and offers – from the sale of books and flowers, to bicycle maintenance and a passion for embroidery – constitutes an element of excellence that often guides the choice of the most experimental young people. Also, the origin and quality of products and ingredients become elements for "taste dispensers" in proposing an original product, based on care and sustainability, which proves to be attractive for ProTasters whose sensitivity seems to be increasingly oriented towards ethics as well as aesthetics.

Gambero Rosso

On December 16th, 1986, a supplement entitled Il Gambero Rosso was published in the newspaper Il manifesto for the first time. The name derives from the legendary tavern where the Cat and the Fox invite Pinocchio to dinner. In 1987, the publishing house Gambero Rosso Editore was created. In 1999, Gambero Rosso became a channel on RaiSat, which in 2009 became the Gambero Rosso Channel. In October 2002, in Rome, the City of Taste was inaugurated, followed by others in Naples, Catania, Palermo, and Turin. These centres of excellence offer cookery courses and expert courses of various kinds. Furthermore, Gambero Rosso manages international projects aimed at promoting Italian excellence abroad.

THE EMBLEMATIC CASE STUDIES

The Gourmet Tea

The Gourmet Tea is a bar and shop dedicated completely to the ritual of drinking tea. The store space is almost a "concept store," with careful management of space focused on design, with bright colours and modern furniture. The packaging of the 35 different types of tea offered by The Gourmet Tea combines simplicity with the power of colour, creating a pleasant contrast with the white walls. The tea is one hundred per cent organic and they can be sampled on site, served at the table on a tray with a transparent teapot filled with hot water and a timer for the correct infusion. Sweet or savoury biscuits, fragrant fruitcakes and other small snacks, all prepared with fresh organic ingredients, are offered to eat alongside the tea.

Iki Care Ceremony

The world of cosmetics and wellbeing has started to offer projects suggesting new models and alternative practices that can enrich the simple act of taking care of oneself for those seeking to experience spatial-temporal moments of great density. The project IKI CARE CEREMONY, launched by Angela Lagana, has its conceptual roots in the Japanese philosophy IKI (hence the name). "Honour your body to nourish the soul" is the ambitious promise of this project. More than a simple line of products, IKI offers a wide range of kits that introduce the concept of at-home rituals and provide a rewarding multi-sensory experience. The high quality of each product is made unique by the various mixtures beyond simple functionality; they become real ceremonies for the Self.

Progetto *Dear Data*

The two protagonists of the project are Giorgia Lupi and Stefanie Posavec, two thirty-six-year-old information designers with no siblings who both crossed the ocean to emigrate and have an artisanal approach to digital work. They met at the EYEO festival, one of the major digital art festivals, and discovered they led the same life but in different places. As a result, they decided to rapidly "process" their lives and tastes for a year and compile the results in infographics. The objective was to discover "the tastes" which they have in common, from music to their emotions, and from their wardrobe to their choice of books. The process included the archiving of data collected in a notebook and their re-elaboration, with pencils and markers on a postcard. Each sent their work to the other. The data became symbols, lines, a colourful world, made of new and different forms, each with a specific meaning. It also includes an alphabet that remains secret until one turns to the back of the postcard with the key for interpreting. A total of 52 postcards are today available on the website created by the two authors: dear-data.com.

Almond

The American platform, active in an alpha version since May 2014, offers the advice of nutritionists and certified experts RD (Registered Dieticians) through one-to-one video-chat meetings instead of in person. Almond offers a series of 30 minute video-meetings, generally a minimum of 2 to 4, via a smartphone, tablet or computer, to review your diet with the aim of losing weight or feeling better and preparing for sports. In the first meeting, the nutritionist collects information on your health and personal lifestyle to create a personalized nutritional plan on which to work though during subsequent meetings, timetabled initially for every 2-3 weeks, then every 3-4. The plan is thus adapted to personal taste preferences, improved and enriched with tactical advice, recipes and different ingredients. Thanks to the app the customer keeps his own nutritionist up to date with the progress made and the nutritionist provides a weekly diet program, and gives specific advice on restaurants and food on offer in the area where the customer lives.

ProTasters

Consumption as

- Sensory richness as a priority in the choices of products and services to take advantage of.
- A means to translate ones own emotions into aesthetics and taste, to recognize quality of life.
- Appreciation of refined products not only aesthetically, able to revisit rituals and occasions.

Communication as

- The search for reference points that direct one's own power for creative expression.
- The valorisation of the magical and emotional side of the experience.
- Discreet refined and empathetic style and language.

Retail as

- Space to promote opportunities for relaxation, especially through soft sensory stimulation.
- The issue/selection of objects, services and concepts with a style and an original point of view. Personalized and rewarding services, even in the smallest detail.

Strategic guidelines

- **Consider** sensory gratification as a tool for cultural enrichment and as a source of deepening personal potential.
- **Propose** products and services, that define new languages and aesthetic codes, increasing the attractiveness by enhancing sensory aspects (graphic, tactile, visual), with refinement.
- **Pamper** interlocutors with dedicated services, and micro-projects oriented towards wellness.
- **Structure** the stores not only as places to make purchases, but also as sensory and emotional experiences, with integrated technologies.
- **Target** a care for architectural details and design, defining an almost labyrinthine structure to the store, punctuated by small, refined and emotional "surprises."

Part Three

The mature adults

The generation X of post-idealists

This third section is dedicated to the more mature adults that we define as post-ideological because today they represent the generational dimension that has personally experienced true "ideological detoxification." They are interpreters of a dimension in which, for the first time, individual existence is made of personal exceptions, not by trends or movements with shared and exclusive values. Their normality is not passive, nor conformist, but formed by their character and personal profile, by couples and professional groups, beyond the strong ideological influence that characterized the previous generation: the Baby Boomers. Also for this reason we have defined them as Generation X, as in Douglas Coupland's book[1] that defined an era, and which describes a generation as "incognito" engaged in reflection on themselves and their own destiny, following the ideological hangovers of the 1960's and 1970's. Born in 1961 immediately after the Baby Boomers, Coupland explores – in this and his other books *Shampoo Planet* and *Microserfs*[2] – the reality experienced by his generation intensively bombarded by the media system still impregnated with the logic of broadcasting, but failing as the ideal vocation between religious crisis, the collapse of ideologies and economic instability that for the first time since the war emerges with increasing regularity.

The Premium Seekers are those who have contrasted ideology with the obsessive pursuit of excellence and tangible quality, to find the source of well being. With financial resources acquired often from the privilege of a

---

[1] Coupland, *op. cit.*
[2] Douglas Coupland, *Microserfs*, Regan Books, New York, 1995; *Shampoo Planet*, Pocket Books, New York, 1992.

long working life, they are seekers of excellence which reward and increase their quality of life, and the last bastions and supporters of material goods, pursued with care and attention moving towards a consumer who qualifies in terms of status.

The Singular Women have instead turned a passion and civil vocation into a solid presence in the social and family sphere, distilling the values that once came from political and ideological commitment. Their uniqueness expresses everything in a proud affirmation of a matured thought that finds everyday realization in the way of managing their multitasking activities with free-thinking pragmatism: in raising children, their professional career, and in solidarity with their community.

In turn, the Mind Builders have metabolized values and behaviours that for some decades have enriched the evolution of advanced services, preparing the ground for the emerging knowledge economy, defining new information protocols, vocational training, social languages, and working in the media, creative agencies, and in the world of teaching and university. Symbolically they accompanied the gradual transition from the pure celebration of the body and self-image – the bodybuilding phase – to the rise of the new and intellectual power of design thinking, which now shows all its relevance by making the cosmopolitan emergence of the ConsumAuthors possible.

Lastly the New Normals, who are the first generation nucleus able to transform television from a uniform container of approved and repeated behaviours, into a workshop of shared uniqueness. It is with them that the very meaning of opposing ideologies and the permanent struggle between right-wing and left-wing values is transformed into a mix of stimuli from which to draw, in a free and personal way; a patchwork that is impossible to interpret according to the classical schemes of politics and ideology.

New Normals

The New Normals constitute the generational nucleus born between the mid 1970's and the first half of the 1980's, at a time of full transition from the ideologies of social movements that had marked the previous decade, to a dimension in which the consumer society of fashion and image had instead taken over. In Italy, this change was defined as "the reflux," marked by the great return of the private sector and "Reagan hedonism," according to the brilliant definition by Roberto d'Agostino in his blog Dagospia, the cantor of the new normal with all its nuances[3]. (Roberto D'Agostino, Cafonal). The formation of this nucleus has followed the evolution of the great television shows like *Saturday Night Live* in the United States that started gaining momentum in the mid-1970's with the release of the Blues Brothers; or in Italy with broadcasts by Renzo Arbore who debuted L'altra domenica in 1976, and *Quelli della notte* in 1985 and that find their consecration with *Indietro tutta* that closed the cycle in 1987-1988. They constructed a television language that differs from the classical view of the silent colourless majority, seeking mediocrity to embrace the idea of a new bewildering and irresistible creativity, appreciated across the board and built according to popular logics and not elitist or niche.

The New Normals aged between 40-50 years represent the classical

---

[3] Roberto D'Agostino, *Cafonal. Gli Italioni nel mirino di Dagospia*, Mondadori, Milan, 2008.

"middle age" subjects. They are very important because, sociologically, they mirror social imaginary and are the link between young and more mature: in this way they re-imagine the mainstream of society. In a historical moment in which information, incentives and continuous stylistic demands promote a kind of aesthetic bulimia that involves large consumption, today an important counter-trend is born with them that develops a search for a new, more sophisticated normality. This has nothing to do with minimalism or diminishing quality, but rather the distillation of taste, offering endless nuances. The concept of beauty for this generational nucleus is played out in details: a difficult challenge that requires skill and great experience.

Having arrived to an understanding of normality as exogenous and not endogenous, through free choice and not social conformity, often the New Normals' reality is made up of exceptions, unique characteristics (just like those chosen by Arbore for his broadcasts, from Benigni to Frassica) on the margins and in the past not accepted: we are in the presence of a new intensity of the normal. For example, they are those who, for over forty years, have adopted the custom of tattooing, only considered a mark of transgression a few years ago. In Italy, 30% of the estimated 7 million people with tattoos only became interested in skin decoration of this type when their years of recklessness had passed. The phenomenon is more prevalent among women: 30% declared to have a tattoo because "they like it," 27% to immortalize dates and names, 9% because it is fashionable and 4% for transgression. For the New Normals, tattoos are a simple means of communication: their generation is the first that began to use them as a form of self-expression, adding more becomes a kind of identity updating. Tattsoo are a modality they have found to tell the world who they are, according to a logic of recognition, not fashion. Even as an adult, every life experience – for example, the birth of a child, that often happens at this age – needs to be recorded and shown to others, maybe on the beach or in the gym. The era of great generational conflicts that characterized the generation immediately preceding theirs, of narcissism and visibility in the society in which they grew up is over. To work on the body becomes a form of storytelling in which skin becomes a kind of blackboard through which to give visibility to intimate aspects of oneself.

Grown up with the reassuring influence of television imaginary, the New Normals lived with the explosion of commercial television and the advent of the New Economy as an opportunity waiting to be exploited.

They are constantly looking for personal satisfaction, through practical life strategies: from politics and economics, to everyday choices and consumption. This nucleus embodies a generation that, for biography, aspiration and commitment, looks to integration between the individual and social dimensions. It is also because of this that they often publish happy moments, sometimes involving their children, on Facebook. They want to tell happy stories and know that the digital space will serve as an inexorable archive. They do it with Family Vlogs: describing how to live a normal domestic existence in the shadow of YouTube. For example, the Shaytard's – a family of vloggers followed by many in the USA, with 3 million subscribers on their YouTube channel and 2 billion views in 5 years. Or the Bratayley's – the second most popular of US vloggers – who have two children, live in Maryland and have filmed every single day for the past 5 years.

Although all studies of this generational nucleus show only a slightly visible change in social expressions, these changes are very important in terms of influencing the mainstream's desires or preferences in their own lives and in family consumption. The New Normals, for example, associate professional success to a rewarding job, a motivation that today is more important than career status or salary. They are aware of being middle aged and that they may never leave their mark from a point of view of symbolic importance, because they often find themselves having to emulate and absorb behaviours of other generations, such as erotic messaging typical of those in their thirties or the simple use of emoticons learned from their children. If teenagers often suffer from adulting, that is, the syndrome of feeling pressured into adult behaviours, the New Normals still seem sensitive to the Peter Pan syndrome, following the path of infantilism, even if playful and informed.

Naturally they also live the dark side of the force, an expression that they absorbed from one of the legends of their teenage years: Star Wars. In particular they suffer from anxiety because of the lack of control they have over the present and guilt due to the difficulty of taking responsibility for the younger generations. According to the National Institute of Mental Health, in the US alone, 20% of the population between 40 and 50 years of age suffers from anxiety disorders such as panic attacks, phobias, post-traumatic stress, and generalized anxiety. The reasons are easy to understand: the infinite number of options that this generation has earned in their personal and professional life, alongside the possibility of daily bric-a-brac, creates a permanent sense of inadequacy. Complete freedom in opinions and behaviour is hard to sustain: it allows the opportunity to achieve their desires but also to worry about possible failures. To this is added the feeling of "mediated fear" greatly increased from September 11th 2001 onwards. In fact, humans are able to associate a sense of danger to objects and situations that have never been a real threat for them. Extending the field of events to a global and connected world inevitably increases emotional mirroring in the most dramatic situations: collective psychology turns into psychosis that the media have a vested interest in amplifying to increase their audience.

The New Normals show themselves to be particularly exposed to the media: some call them postmodernists, those for whom everything is relative, without major roots, in a mix of anxieties and desires. For them, technology also constitutes an irreplaceable life partner, to amplify tastes and passions, and participate in groups that reinforce their identity. To give just a few examples, they represent the nucleus that supports the huge market success of products for pets, the care of their body and personal and family wellbeing. They follow trends but never get involved in extreme phenomena. At one time it seemed that they belonged to the silent majority but today it would be wrong to reduce them toward a dimension of middle class conformism from which they also come: rather they elaborated and metabolized the evolution of the time in which they live in a "normal" way.

In the moment in which lifestyles and consolidated categories of consumption fall, the New Normals rely on a relationship with objects attributable more to the logic of "collectibles" than status, to master the world and master time, interrupting and classifying them in the same way as habits, and following their passions. The practice of collecting affirms their freedom of taste; it is a place to express their individuality as well as their eccentricities, to escape bureaucratic structures and contingent obligations. Once again, the logic of a normality made up of exceptions emerges.

New Normals made the battles on civil rights their own; they favour civil unions and are tolerant of diversity. In some cases, they have embraced controlled diets, casual elegance at work and sportswear in their spare time. Fitness and health consciousness have marked the path, like in the fashion industry of the 1980's, the star system in the 1990's, the new economy in the year 2000 and great economic crisis in 2007. Master Chef, blogs and weekends away in cities searching for art or hunting for food and wine experiences, still today mark their presence in the world of consumption.

They are the great supporters of happy life occasions, even if few and far between: intense, nominal pleasure is their daily bread, to counteract the depressive threat of global tragedies. In this regard the Google campaign dedicated to micro-moments is emblematic: to remember, celebrate, share, moments from which to extract the maximum satisfaction and personal growth.

Professional future: Distributors of health and beauty

The professions at the heart of our liquid society – "disbanded" because of the increasingly frantic movement of people who are disengaged from traditional dynamics and status – are those with an elevated *human touch*. In the challenge of building the future, it is vital learning how to professionally handle the increased warmth of human relations. Online and offline: the web and social networks generate heat and "social physics," as Alex Pentland states in his book of the same title[4], exponentially increasing the number of contacts and exchanges with our friends or digital followers. These connections very often correspond to people that we know, appreciate and listen to. The normal dimensions of human existence, those linked to the body, health and seduction, are also those who engage in delicate relationship dynamics, both in digital interpersonal care and mutual recognition.

For the New Normals all of this becomes essential, a life priority. For this way of life we must develop talents and skills in the renewed dimension of ever more emotional personal services: not only doctors but also trainers, tattooists and dieticians. For professions of the future, to "create value" will correspond to the art of caring for customers, guaranteeing the delicate construction of human relationships. We must transmit competence but also "human warmth," reinforcing the sense of recognition and gratitude.

They must learn the artisan form of "normal" care, exercised with subtle grace, creativity and imagination. As shown the success of the Italian series *Braccialetti rossi*, which casts sick patients of a hospital ward as the heroes. Or the success of a French movie like *La Famille Bélier*, which

---

[4] Alex Pentland, *Social Physics: How Good Ideas Spread – The Lessons from a New Science*, Penguin, New York, 2014.

treats with great irony the condition of an able-bodied girl as part of a deaf family. Even in these cases of the new normal – made up of exceptions – "human warmth" always wins.

Jawbone Up

"Once you try it you don't want to be without. Because it takes care of your physique and your mood, even when you sleep. Its better than a relationship." This is what Matteo Bordone wrote a few years ago on Wired Italia to describe his "symbiosis" with the Jawbone Up bracelet, that keeps track of the physical activity of the wearer through its sensors. Based in San Francisco and founded by two students from Stanford University, it is considered one of the most innovative companies in the world. Jawbone Up allows you to better understand your health and improve your lifestyle, thanks to analysis of sleep-related data, movement and nutrition. The more you use it, the more sophisticated its understanding and interaction becomes, with invitations to pursue a suggested target.

THE EMBLEMATIC CASE STUDIES

The Museum of Me

Social networks tell many stories of millions of people's live, but digital memory tends to be short-term. Many initiatives are being developed that focus on rendering our past virtual social relations tangible and visible. The Museum of Me by Intel is an application that (after authorization from the user) collects information from one's Facebook Page in order to create a video that turns friends, text, images and keywords into a virtual journey within an imaginary museum – all of which is dedicated to the story of "me." In a similar way, Social Memories by Deutsche Post allows you to create and print a real book, full of images, data and statistics that puts our digital life into black and white.

Brand New China

Conceived by Hong Huang, a veteran from the world of media and communication, and author of a blog followed by over 800,000 fans, BNC (Brand New China) is the new platform for young Chinese designers, artists and stylists. The project took shape in 2010, with the opening of a large exhibition space where objects, furniture, accessories and garments of excellence are presented and sold, with one key difference: instead of dealing with "classic" luxury products, refined unique pieces with a clear local image were displayed that best represents the new Chinese creative identity. The boutique reflects these new values through a bold selection that mixes different styles, ranging from street wear to the most experimental jewellery. The ambition of the project is to create a laboratory that is able to generate new aesthetic trends beyond the prevalent Western-style and to export this vision beyond Chinese borders.

House of Hackney

British homes are places where the most elaborate wallpaper designs and an extensive use of carpeting is used, representing a true cultural archetype. In the Nineties, the new generations adopted a more minimalistic and cold style, radically abandoning the tradition of covering walls. In the first decade of the new millennium, a renewed desire for decorative glory together with a growing air of nostalgia created an opening for this surviving sensibility, which the House of Hackney is taking full advantage of. Founded in 2010 as an interior design label, the brand re-proposes the concept of complete wall coverings, through textiles and prints on paper that re-interpret designs from the Victorian era often in a humorous and irreverent way. Today, the House of Hackney has evolved, incorporating its interior design with fashion and lifestyle divisions, including collections featuring floral and animal prints with unusual colours and used in original ways.

Haolilai

Haolilai is one of the most well known brands of snacks in China and in recent years has considerably extended its range of crisps in tubes, similar to the famous Pringles. The line Potato Wish offers crisps that are baked not fried and without unsaturated fat or additives, trying to prevent concerns about one's figure and health, both priorities for the Chinese public. In fact, snacks are often linked to the idea of female beauty: a sweet, fragile women who feeds herself on small daily treats, for example. Some of the advertising for the new snack Potato Wish promotes the idea of cooking as a game: creative recipes are suggested in which the crisps become the main ingredient in preparing a tasty and original snack, such as a "castle of crisps with mashed potatoes."

New Normals

Consumption as

- The integration of everyday experiences, for a real and virtual relationship without solution of continuity.
- Recognition of uniqueness, with increasingly exclusive forms of customization.
- Continual research of excellent experiences, even in the physical spaces of retail.

Communication as

- Proposal for an update on the coolest news.
- The preview of dedicated services, of a single brand or in partnership.
- Services that focus on timeliness for life occasions, also within 24 hours.

Retail as

- Places with products and experiences geared to meet the desire to "everything new."
- Time for experiences, discoveries, adventures to explore in person, in town, on vacation, travelling, with personalized alert, linked to the territory.
- Projects and products that enrich and make the retail space unique, through art and design.

Strategic guidelines

- **Reason** on innovative forms of the new normal.
- **Define** products and services for the regenerated condition of middle age.
- **Propose** increasingly effective responses to shared and common needs.
- **Adopt** forms of communication and promotion in which widespread excellence emerges.
- **Intercept** the collective imaginary with ideas adapted to different occasions.

Singular Women

"I'm not single but I feel singular in my choices"

(40-60 year old, females)

The Singular Women were born in the 1960's, at the height of the feminist wave, shaping – at a very young age – the great civil rights battles, from Martin Luther King in the USA and the conquest of abortion and divorce in Italy. Women between 40 and 60 years of age who are increasingly aware and self-confident and who highlight the importance of their hard-won independence in their life and consumption choices. They work on the awareness of their organizational abilities, on human charge, supporting new civil and valorial issues. In part, the trend coincides with ta weakening of the male identity in developed societies and, in parallel, the consolidation of a "feminine imprint" from aspects of daily life and family care, now extended to the workplace and issues that affect all of society. The singularity of their existence is shown by the increasingly high rate of female subjects able to take charge in all areas under their responsibility.

The Singular Women who express their feminine singularity are increasingly bold women, self-confident, and aware of their own strength. Their emergence in the 1980's and 1990's also coincided with the weakening of the male aesthetic identity. Over the past 20 years there has been much discussion of a *single* condition, which has been considered the new socio-demographic perspective in future society. In reality, behind this demographic data, a more complex reality was often hidden, made up of cohabitation and non-institutional partnerships, and moving away from mere "isolationist" individualism on which the character of the *single* of the 1990's was built, and that the media system defined in the years of transition between the second and third millennium.

For the Singular Women the sense of awareness and utility of culture with an ethical, social and civil scope grows and strengthens. Philosophical thinking makes a constructive criticism towards the media, technology and progress in general, highlighting the importance of personal growth. In the complex and continuous process of these women's personality formation leisure time is lived as an important container of experiences in which they experiment with alternative paths, complementary to work activities, in order to stimulate personal growth. This generational nucleus targets the core of things in search for deep authenticity.

The Singular Women creatively interpret the values of the society they live in, translating them into life and consumption choices, both minimum and complex, selecting and activating organizational systems for themselves and their family. By working on individual awareness, and rewarding human energy and value, they are able to promote issues related to work and family management, and open-up wider issues that are relavent to the whole society. This mature and aware female world lives the present and its opportunities passionately in search of new equilibriums, to understand the complex existential dynamics, and to look for real solutions to improve their life and that of others. For them, there is no clear division between the good and the beautiful; they show a great desire to see a fair and righteous world that is also a pleasant environment which brings together creative energy and critical reflection.

In the world of communication, *Sex & The City* for some years shaped the imaginary generational reference for these women, while in reality new forms of relationships and sharing flourished between the extended family and the female character. A few years later this supported the success of *Desperate Housewives*, for example. The freedom to live with the joy and sensuality of their bodies and their relationship with everyday life, beyond age and agreed aesthetic canons, is influencing this feminine dimension.

The Singular Women work on the awareness of their abilities, on human energy and values, supporting new aesthetics and introducing, at the same time, themes related to work and family management, as well as everyday feelings and actions, from home and work to broader issues affecting society as a whole. This is not about competing with the masculine, nor is it a mere assertion of rights: this all female generational nucleus simply embodies a different point of view through their own consumption and life choices *tout court*.

For them it is vital to keep stereotypes alive as a way to fill everyday life with energy and fun: openly overthrowing, with irony and lightness, the old game between seduction and power, and emphasizing the most critical and sensitive issues, such as violence against women.

In relation to this generational nucleus, South and Central America are important areas for the production and dissemination of an increasingly autonomous and original creativity. In these countries the role of the body and its deepest expressions is finally freeing itself from the "touristic" dimension of folklore (or sexual tourism), and acquiring a unique and universal relevance.

The spreading of a Singular Woman identity shows the importance of a dynamic linked to female independence that – starting from 35 years of age – works on the critical values of "singularity." It does not end in the state of being single but proposes a type of thought and behaviour upon which even the masculine world begins to face. Together with Latin America, the Middle East, the Far East and Northern Europe are also sensitive to and active in developing new codes of female behaviour, despite their differences.

"Life Simplification" is the main keyword in which the female world has always had a fundamental design role, working on emerging values, quality and materials, creative processes and uniqueness. For this reason, Singular Women's successful production and distribution strategies are able to combine high quality design with the centrality of relationships and the articulation of services. In this context, uniqueness is not considered a static characteristic, but a strategic vision that develops and builds on a solid conceptual basis that is constantly updated. The Singular Women appreciate projects that trigger a process of constant reflection on new values, through aesthetic fruition and innovative proposals.

In particular, the female world seems to live the present with more intensity, opportunities and problems, and it is from these issues that it wants to restart. This aptitude and sensitivity continues to fuel alternative behaviours. The idea of community and shared interests, passions and life issues, for example, is convincing and is transformed into tangible and highly proactive realities, understood as open entities, free to organize themselves around specific needs. The companies and associations that carefully consider the creative potential produced by the female world multiply, supporting desires and giving a voice to their needs usually online.

From the point of view of corporate projects for the Singular Women, the Campaign for Real Beauty promoted by Dove, a Unilever corporation brand, is exemplary. Dove's advertisements refer to ordinary women and thus promote an attainable feminine ideal, close to the experience of all women. The campaign, thanks to it unusual subjects, was a great international success and continued over time, going well beyond pure advertising. By funding research on the perception of beauty, came the idea to create the "Dove Self-Esteem Fund."

Professional future: The bio-developer

In the future Singular Women professions that work closely with the logic and rules of biology will become more common, without necessarily having to know the secrets. The role of bio-developer does not merely concern the most sophisticated analysis of biological engineering and medical research, but also experimentation that, for example with food design or formal research linked to textiles, increasingly shifts the world of aesthetics and expressive languages. The great novelty concerns the variety of increasingly bold possible applications and professions that deal with the living world from different points of view. Microbiologists will collaborate with set designers, farmers with the most sophisticated chefs, because everyone will have to compete with the recipes of life, just as the Singular Women do so well. Moreover the humanistic exploration of knowledge over time tends to integrate with the scientific acquisition of Big Data.

What once corresponded to a scientific specialization, today translates into a range of possibilities running through all sectors: from organic food and naturalist tourism, to holistic medicine and bio-architecture, and from organic clothing to the study of new materials. All this will turn many of us into bio-developers. In this way, the biological dimension will gain a basic understanding, and will be considered in many different subjects beyond this vocation, recovering the extraordinary experience of Leonardo da Vinci, the first to have understood the importance of the science of life. In this future perspective, the term "bio" will no longer be just a prefix of fashion, but the basis for business and consumer-related projects, based on economic models studied, for example, by Gunter Pauli, in his book *The Blue Economy*, in collaboration with scientists, institutional partners, public and private bodies.

UpCycle and GroCycle

UpCycle in France and GroCycle in the UK are two start-ups founded by young entrepreneurs who have developed urban mushroom factories by exploiting the nutritional power of something that was considered only waste: coffee grounds. After collecting the initial investment through crowd founding, UpCycle and GroCycle created a truly integrated system in their respective local areas, collecting unwanted coffee grounds and producing mushrooms to be distributed in bulk or in a kit. The two start-ups have been successful by turning waste into consumer products and harnessing otherwise waste materials such as coffee grounds and under-utilized human resources. They are now seeking new partners.

THE EMBLEMATIC CASE STUDIES

Tanita Shokudo

The opening in Tokyo in January 2012 of Tanita Shokudo, a "nutritionist" restaurant, has prompted a serious public debate in Japan devoted to health, food and science. Tanita Corp., who specializes in producing electronic devices dedicated to health and wellbeing, launched the project. In the Tanita Shokudo restaurant, the recipes originate from the company's own cookbook, in which refined Japanese menus were developed containing a maximum of 500 calories. The aesthetics of the space draws inspiration from a hospital: each table has a scale to weigh the contents of each plate, while a timer indicates the optimal duration of the meal. Before sitting at a table and ordering, the clients can enter a separate room where professional dieticians will provide a free consultation and define an ideal diet after a detailed examination.

Story

In February 2012, Story opened in the Meatpacking District of New York: a space for retail but above all experiences conceived by the former marketing consultant, Rachel Shechtman. Following a theme that acts as a common thread, every 4/8 weeks the space changes "skin," renewing installations, furnishings and the type of goods sold. According to the creator, Story offers the perspective of a magazine, the composition of a gallery and trades like a store. It is a true, all-round experience for the visitor who can visit the space as a client/consumer, as a student of the various organized workshops, or as the mere spectator of an "exhibition" that is renewed with each installation. Story is a way for the founder to share her passions that lie somewhere between shopping and culture.

Pierette res capillorum

In Berlin is the particularly interesting Salon Pierette res capillorum of Mulackstrasse, which defines itself as "Haarschneiderei" literally "hair couture" (in German the *Erei* suffix indicates the traditional approach). It is an example of how small local businesses can meet with the growing need from advanced consumers for a well-balanced mix of excellence and honesty. The owner of this Salon has chosen to go against the tide of the sector, which often uses aggressive performative products and treatments on the hair. Instead, it proposes a service made up of natural products, freshly prepared colours and cuts that, although can take up to two hours, last and enhance the natural beauty of each client. To highlight how the activity is totally "a work of art," within the salon there are art journals, not the usual glossy fashion or beauty magazines.

Kuku Design

Around the world the number of design studios engaged in activities linked to a basic and almost handmade creative sustainability is multiplying. These studios want to bring consumers closer with the simplicity of proposals and with a solid educational approach, close to the sharing of craft workshops that aim to bring design to ordinary people. Among the many cases, we have selected Kuku Design in Buenos Aires: a studio with its own brand, offering projects and products that go to the heart of creative recycling. Kuku holds regular meetings in order to exchange and collect waste materials that can be converted into new products. Kuku's objects are small containers made from PET bottles, light bulbs and glass vials, but also drinking glasses cut from the base of bottles and "organic vases" created using eggshells: a minimalistic and ironic world of domestic design.

Singular Women

Consumption as

- The affirmation of one's own uniqueness and autonomy.
- Activities managed and organized in detail with a selective approach to the market.
- Sensibility to original and useful proposals, oriented from smart solutions.

Communication as

- Mirror of independence and critical thinking .
- Media imaginary of reference always in search of new forms of relations and sharing.
- The search for new languages, filtered by an intelligent and creative pragmatism.

Retail as

- A place that offers a critical view of consumption, distant from worlds and installations perceived as too cool.
- Platforms for active and shared participation, which leverage the unique strengths of "differences." A sales point with an articulated service, where "informative and educational vocation" prevail.

Strategic guidelines

- **Be** rigorous in ethical choices and visions, proposed on products, services and communication in a transparent and inclusive manner.
- **Target** the pleasantness and the aesthetics of products that find both simplicity of operation and immediacy of use at the same time.
- **Propose** new services in a concrete and everyday context, to help in a practical manner women better manage the complexity of everyday life.
- **Use** point of sale as the perfect place to recount their projects: showing them and sharing objectives.
- **Starting** from the brand's credibility, offer a highly specialized service in which an "educational-formative" vocation shared with customers prevails.

Mind Builders

The Mind Builders are a generational nucleus that represents an expression of cosmopolitan intellectual bourgeoisie, with a vocation for knowledge expressed in all its forms. Born and raised in the 1960's, they are the younger and more forward thinking point of the Baby Boomers. They stand out because of their search for a personal point of view, as an intellectual exercise, in conjunction marking the growth of the Web and passage of the millennium. From bodybuilding of the 1980's and1990's, they brought us mind building of the new age by becoming digital immigrants. The short circuit between what is considered essential and the dynamic of deep reflection on the meaning of existence, led to the emergence of a new "philosophy of life": the Mind Builders are contemporary existentialists, who embody and experience this new adventure. Lovers of thought and a new cultural dimension without disciplinary boundaries or borders, they are new cosmopolitan intellectuals and technologists, but also proud of their roots and links to the territory. They are the lovers of languages in all their versions and of intercultural exchange. The Mind Builders are therefore very advanced from an intellectual, cultural and economic point of view: true digital immigrants living with great cultural continuity, they have the opportunities of the digital world without departing from an elevated view of the quality and importance of content which has, for example, re-launched investigative journalism with the success of the Oscar-winning film, Spotlight. Their choices are driven by a strong need for knowledge in all fields, with a regenerated relationship between theory and practice.

This generational nucleus is strongly attracted by the chance to new approaches in art, science, and philosophy and other areas of knowledge, with a strong professional connotation. We can speak of a true *forma mentis*, which is linked to a genuine and natural interest in exploring their creative and intellectual potential. The status of the Mind Builders is therefore spontaneous, creative, open to change and bound to constant training, if not a challenge that runs through their talents and passions. The demonstration of these values use very refined aesthetic codes of communication. The short circuit between creative energy and critical thinking, along with characteristic traits of this group, promotes the continued emergence of new forms of expression.

For Mind Builders, the key word is personality. The brain is a complex organ that regulates and balances the functions of the entire human organism. If well "trained," with exercises and the most appropriate intellectual stimulation, a strong personality can be constructed. Thought, increasingly rapid and dynamic, is perceived as the engine for behaviours and choices, individual and collective. Mind Builders strongly attracted by smart objects that encompass the value of an advanced technological research and guarantee exclusive performance. The Mind Builders love to be engaged in interactive services, demonstrations of technological advancement and aesthetic research, which also contain a playful component. They are enthusiasts of integral experiences and a new reflexive awareness: architects, computer scientists, journalists and administrators, heavily involved in Smart Cities projects that are shaping the new urban experience worldwide.

In the daily lives of this generation, food proves to be a new field of interest, for its ability to also determine intellectual growth: in many areas, from ethnic cuisine to creative experimentation, led by the great chefs. In this perspective, their participation in projects such as Eataly (the successful business created by Oscar Farinetti, conceived as a relational platform directed towards the general public, for small medium scale producers of Italian food excellence, otherwise destined to remain in a small niche), where consumption is just one of the elements involved, becoming the source of a type of knowledge that creates innovation and competence, giving added value to the purchase.

Among the contexts of life, the multi-ethnic city becomes the protagonist of experiences but also the imaginary. The cosmopolitan approach of the Mind Builders with their interest in exchange between cultures, markets and minds, leads them naturally to an interest in urban opportunities for sharing, in which the experiences of wellbeing, fun or consumption are far from solitary. The originality of the cultural mix also brings the Mind Builders to live their origins as a means for dialogue: expanding their culture becomes possible for the first time. To participate in the market of cross-cultural exchange expands the boundaries of personal experience and opens the possibility for collective change.

In the worlds of work, study, and especially that of consumption, the Mind Builders are seeking paths to follow without a precise destination, but that simply enhance the value the journey, the experience and growth. In this sense, the mythical principle of six degrees of separation originated and guaranteed the success of Linkedin – an online social networking service founded by Reid Hoffman, mainly used for professional purposes. The Linkedin network has millions of users in North America, Asia and Europe and has for many years grown at a rate of 100,000 subscribers per week.

The search for a personal point of view causes the Mind Builders to feed on travel, in the physical and not just metaphorical sense, as a privileged source of knowledge and inspiration. While traveling they explore their creative and intellectual potential, and express their desire to be part of the cosmopolitan elite. The status of the Mind Builder is therefore spontaneous, creative, yet open to change and bound to constant training. The expression of these values uses highly refined aesthetics and codes of communication, that are measured with the idea of "world travel."

This group is perhaps the most able to simultaneously enjoy the inter-cultural charm of the global product and the excellence of the local artefact, that they recognize with great expertise. This type of traveller has a strong need to share "iconic narratives" based on stories of people, places and excellent cult products. Journeys for them become stories.

They define the taste experience on the basis of value-priorities, quality of life, and knowledge of the territory as well as the specific cultures. Elements from the sphere of knowledge are transferred to the everyday consumer. The driving factor and magnetic pole for Mind Builders is everything that reveals its nature and original character. Proposals and paths made possible by a careful cognitive rigor and by the implementation of processes and creative practices. Perpetrators and accomplices of an ever-new design culture, they wish to express their views in a realistic and direct way. Culture is never separated from a specific knowledge of materials, functions and the compositions of everyday objects. The mix between cosmopolitan tension and consciousness of their roots constitutes a generative strength. Spaces and contexts in tune with this sensitivity are appreciated, beyond trends and stereotypes. Elements from the sphere of knowledge are transferred to the everyday consumer.

Professional future: Explo-Teachers

The digital revolution will change the role of teachers; this is a transformation that the Mind Builders are able to metabolize. It will not manifest itself as a generational conflict, but as a process of convergence between the different generational skills: exploration, speed, collaboration, and planning. In this situation the professions and the activities related to teaching will profoundly change: within universities large areas will open up to those who can teach, reconciling the transfer of knowledge with new, less prescriptive and more exploratory, experience models. Teachers and applications emerge with new skills, accompanied by a spirit of adventure that future generations appreciate. In one sense, the professions related to teaching will have to master the classic approach of the "experienced teacher." Take the case of University: 9 out of 10 university students own a smartphone and have a Facebook profile. Students continuously communicate on the Web in their daily lives, except when they begin studying at university, which should be a place of innovation. Students and teachers are connected via email, but lessons, learning and exams take place in an analogue mode. The gap between analogue and digital is substantial, for a leap into the future that looks to technology and the development of the digital as a service to easily enrich lives as well as teaching and learning. Simplification that becomes democratic access to educational of excellence for all is the path to imagine new activities and professions. For future training, technology will be a key tool for improving education and gaining access to shared and creative learning. This does not preclude the validity of lectures: for students, listening to a professor remains a staple of learning, provided that it is supported by a captivating language and an inspirational vision. It requires that teachers – many of who represent the nucleus of the Mind Builders – return to being teachers of life.

Duolingo

Duolingo is a free app for learning languages. The business model is simple and innovative: the user can learn a foreign language and in exchange – when the reach a high level of learning – translate short sentences. The translated texts are then corrected and rated by other users. In this way Duolingo is able to sell translations for websites, including CNN and BuzzFeed. The founder is Luis Von Ahn, known for having invented reCAPTCHA and CAPTCHA, the well-known systems that block net bots and, at the same time, help to digitalise books in a unique collaboration between man and machine in order to decode cultural content. Two independent studies by the City University of New York and the University of South Carolina have shown that the degree of learning through Duolingo is superior to that of a university language course. In 2013, Apple chose it as "App of the Year," bestowing for the first time the prestigious award to an app dedicated to education.

THE EMBLEMATIC CASE STUDIES

House Kombucha

House Kombucha is a small local business reviving the ancient Japanese tradition of fermenting raw tea; a complicated probiotic drink made from local ingredients, without sugar or added flavours. The company is owned and operated by a group of young people from San Francisco, involved not only in the production of a natural and artisanal drink, but also in the local community. Working from a factory in the city centre, House Kombucha inspires and enriches the community not only commercially, but facilitates the retrieval and reuse of its bottles (an energy saving 17 times greater than simple glass recycling). When the customer returns the bottle to the store, they are not only helping this local business but also helping to foster closer relations.

Local Motors

Local Motors is an American company that produces made-to-order cars, fulfilling the desires of customers who want to manage the design process. The company adopts a unique approach to design, that of "co-creation," combined with a revolutionary assemblage and sales system on a local basis, using the principles of crowd sourcing to design and develop vehicles in a collaborative manner with the involvement of an open community of designers and potential clients. The assembly of the vehicles takes place in various workshops scattered throughout Massachusetts and Arizona. The customer can follow the construction of their car and is kept informed of its progress by a personal builder trainer. The Rally Fighter is the first vehicle in the world to be created in this "open source" way.

The Sketchbook Project

Founded in 2010 through the work of the Art House University in Atlanta, USA, The Sketchbook Project is a collective project, a touring public space and a community patrimony that continuously grows. It has fast become a benchmark for multimedia artists from over one hundred countries, who have left their mark on Sketchbook by sharing their varied experiences and art that crosses physical and cultural borders. Born as a touring project, in 2011/12 it travelled between the United States, Canada and Europe (London), before permanently locating to the Brooklyn Art Library, in December 2011 in a former spice warehouse renovated ad hoc. The project is open to anyone who wants to share their story, vision or experience, and creates a huge archive of visual inspiration.

FORMAT

In February 2015, the acclaimed creative director, music producer and artist, Trevor Jackson, presented a limited edition of his first album in 14 years: F O R M A T, a celebration of music in physical format. According to Jackson: "Another (story) created by each and everyone, composed by the effort that you put in having purchased an object, in touching it, in the rite you perform every time you start it up." The album includes 12 songs, each recorded on a different media, including 12, 10 and 7 inch vinyl discs, CD, mini CD, audio cassette, USB, videotape, MiniDisc, Digital Audio Tape (DAT), 8-track and reel, all available individually online. The work was also presented with an exhibition at The Vinyl Factory in London, where besides being able to buy and preview the songs, you could watch an audio-visual presentation designed ad hoc by Jackson.

Mind Builders

Consumption as

- The fruition of the product in a cultural key.
- The search for products with a high intellectual content.
- Appreciation of ideas and aesthetics of the past.

Communication as

- Expression of a quality that highlights processes of excellence.
- Knowledge and co-creation on the theme of innovation.
- Sharing of the history and values of a brand, which accords with project sharing.

Retail as

- Space for the exploration of processes and the supply chain.
- The promotion of cultural initiatives, in a kind of extended patronage.
- A place to meet and exchange up to date culture, with on-going insights.

Strategic guidelines

- **Consider** products and services offered by the company (for example, the packaging), primarily as containers of ideas and statements.
- **Bring** creative processes to the heart of the consumption experience.
- **Encourage** the desire to know companies, through stories that tell of their visionary skills, in the future and the past.
- **Produce** the pleasure for co-creation that comes from the stimulation of thought, starting from dialogue.
- **Imagine** stores that are "open" in which to propose a deepening of the knowledge of the company and its products.

Premium Seekers

The Premium Seekers are post World War II children, bearers of a new energy, hope and material wellbeing. In their social life they identify with the concept of prestige and distinction, they have large disposable income and a high level of cultural awareness that drives them in the search for excellence. High quality is not only a status symbol but also an expression of an intrinsic value: quality of life prevails over social representation. The women, who alongside the men, interpret the Premium Seekers' values, are steadily growing around the world. This so-called "feminization" of purchasing power (once this nucleus was comprised only of men and defined as DeLuxe Men) that increasingly values excellence, has moved from the materialistic world to that of services for the body, care and culture.

In recent years, the same physiology of the happy few, namely of the economically privileged global niches, has profoundly changed. Much of the consumption and behaviour that once was practiced by the socio-cultural elite in many countries has spread and extended to an upper-middle class which came to become part of a dimension, previously considered inaccessible (it was luxury for the privileged few), which today has been defined by some as a "necessary luxury." The group of Premium Seekers was born from this epochal change.

This dynamic – particularly present in the West, in the most advanced countries, skilled in the metabolism of consumption – has helped define the same codes of luxury and the profile of that generational nucleus, which gravitates in the context of the more mature 55-70 year olds. For many individuals in this age range, the values of excellence have moved from the materialistic and ostentatious world to services dedicated to the body, wellbeing, and spirit. Time, tranquillity, quality of life, constitute the answer for a restless generation which has experienced well-being and that no longer directly aspires to the classic consumption of luxury. Even in the United States, home to the new billionaires of Silicon Valley the hyperbole of super-luxury is abandoned, while a new class of "working rich" emerges, that despite having a wealth of between 1 and 10 million dollars, have a lifestyle and aspirations of the affluent upper-middle class. There are eight million households living according to a new sobriety of values, which evoke seriousness and prudence. For them the idea is "honest luxury," with consumption, above all linked to health, safety and schooling.

In those countries where capitalism – for different reasons – arrived only a few decades ago (from Russia and China, to Brazil and the United Arab Emirates) with its burden of symbols and products, a privileged class of people has quickly formed – driven by very powerful oligarchies, often linked to the control of energy resources – recognized in the codes and the logics of more traditional luxury. In this case, the DeLuxe Men reside in the construction industry, in finance, and the media, art and politics. This generational nucleus, which identifies with the concept of prestige and distinction, collects all the expressions of a "new real luxury." In Russian high society it is a must, and generally for the new rich the world over, beyond the former emerging markets defined BRIC (Brazil, Russia, India, China). This is a patriarchal world which adopted the aesthetic logics of the 1980's and that is also reflected in the female counterpart of the big brands and theatrical ostentation. We must emphasize, however, that even this group is destined to veer in the direction of the Premium Seekers in a matter of years.

The Premium Seekers belong to the wealthiest 10% of families in a country. For example, in Italy, 45% identify with the concept of prestige and distinction. The lifestyle and consumption habits of this generational group reflect a continuous search for excellence in every field, not to demonstrate their superior status, but to enrich their lives with the best that the market can offer. Quality of life prevails over social status.

The Premium Seekers, which also include the new rich of emerging countries, are globally defined as the adult representatives of high class society worldwide: a generation that knows wellbeing but does not aspire directly to classical luxury consumption and following the crisis, lives according to a new depth of values, with relevant and non-ostentatious consumption, distinctive but not "over the top." For this new elite we can talk of "vocational consumption:" their attention to value for money is accentuated, accompanied by a solid cultural base, making products or services lose their appeal. Even luxury aesthetic codes have changed, bringing creative people to work on original quality, and the Premium Seekers to appreciate a "deluxe simplicity" made up of a few high-quality things; the best, unique and iconic pieces, designer accessories which stand out for their creativity, exuberant but are not excessive.

Substance defeats appearance in the choices of the Premium Seekers, in terms of fashion, design, enogastronomy and tourism. For many subjects of this generation nucleus, the values of excellence have transferred from the materialistic world to services for the body, care and culture.

Women who reach this social status are steadily growing worldwide and in particular in Asian countries where, traditionally, women and trade constituted a well established combination. It is also for this "feminine imprint" that increasingly the world of luxury accompanies classic products, symbols of male purchasing power, with premium services linked to credit cards, exclusive club membership, travel and the most exotic hotels, thus creating a new language of power which includes more and more women.

The values of excellence and quality are the main points of reference for the Premium Seekers in the markets and for Western consumers, who grew up with repeated and sophisticated consumption habits, filtered by thirty years of expertise and experience of everyday life. Excellence and taste mingle with luxury and prestige with the recent experience of the new rich in emerging economies, who in just five years have witnessed, a sudden and focused development of things "good" and "beautiful." In these countries, status, ostentation and privilege find their perfect expression in the new codes of fashion, design, architecture and art, emerging in a mix that seemingly repeats the logic and standards of the eighties, instead of proposing new forms of dynamic excellence, that in aesthetic terms find new paths in an exciting duel between novelty and innovation. In this sense, it is interesting to work on the credibility of aesthetic brands and styles, without settling for a critical review of tradition. For Western companies, it comes down to regenerating the memory of excellence in a manner compatible with the new rich of Eastern countries, alongside re-inventing the standards of quality and excellence to reach their markets.

The ability to recognize and cultivate the uniqueness and extraordinariness of the territory and life occasions renders the Premium Seekers a nucleus of elective reference and, at the same time, careful experimenters in new taste and lifestyles. Travel, cultural and recreational activities, are all designed to meet the need for absolute quality that satisfy the search for 'premium' experiences of an exemplary standard. Personal care is orientated towards the valorization of oneself, a vital sign of individual values. This is a vocational consumption, which selects based on the criteria of substance, duration and sound cultural foundations. Prestigious products and services distinguish this approach, where the top of the range is not only a status symbol, but also an expression of intrinsic value. With this in mind they choose intense places and contexts that become unique and universally recognized.

Professional future: Trainers of excellence

A few years ago – particularly in the world of clothing and fashion accessories – mainly in the United States, the figure of the Personal Shopper, a connoisseur of style and the coolest consumption dynamics, spread. More than just sales assistants who helped wealthy and demanding Department Store customers choose the best clothing, they are true masters of style able to work wonders with the client's image at a glance, from the complexion and colours, to the physical and psychological characteristics of the shoppers. Often they were young Italians to which a natural elegance and an ability to coordinate colour, forms and fabrics together in a flawless look came naturally. Today this professionalism gives way to the "Trainer of excellence" who has extended their reach to include all types of quality consumption: from food and wine, tourism and design, to personal accessories and beauty. Fashion is just one of the dimensions – not even the most important – on which the Premium Seekers construct their consumption experience, requiring an on-going consultancy to ensure the most original and refined choices. Very often all this takes place online through the presence of ever more qualified specialists-bloggers who, with their activities, are able to reach thousands of fans and followers providing style guidance and personalized advice. On the basis of these characteristics their activity can be defined as "Trainer of excellence."

Espace Premiere Lounge

VIP Lounges are now present in airports around the world, though not all offer the same level of service. Some command a breath-taking view (such as the Panorama Lounge in Zurich), others luxury services, exclusiveness and sophisticated design. But among the most prestigious and unique worldwide is the Air France Espace Premiere Lounge located at Charles de Gaulle airport in Paris (also supported by Forbes). Considered to be the best and most modern VIP lounge in Europe, just 37 visitors can use a Spa, private bathrooms with showers, a massage service to help passengers best prepare or recover energy before or after a long-haul flight. A personal assistant is always at hand while a limousine transfers passengers from the lounge to their aircraft where the Air France crew greet them.

THE EMBLEMATIC CASE STUDIES

Schloss Elmau

Schloss Elmau is a five-star resort with a luxury Spa and cultural lodge in Elmau, Southern Germany, on the Austrian border. The excellence of the resort is evident in all the different services. In a breath-taking natural environment, you can spend your leisure time exploring the area, enjoy a wide variety of spa activities or play sports, from golf to Martial Arts. However, the pride of the resort is its cultural offerings: from an elegant library, to the bookstore. Throughout the year, festivals are organized in the beautiful concert hall, such as the jazz festival in May, or the musical symposia organized by prestigious international associations.

Hearts and Crafts

The French fashion house Hermès decided to pay tribute to its artisans through a series of short video portraits of their master craftsmen. The end result is *Hearts and Crafts. The people that make Hermès*, a refined documentary directed by Frédéric Laffont and Isabelle Dupuy-Chavanat in 2011. The idea was to emphasize the incredible work that makes the creation of each individual product of its vast collection unique. Throughout France, from Paris to the Ardennes, from the Lyon to Lorraine, master craftsmen of all ages opened the doors of their workshops to tell their life story and celebrate their almost obsessive passion and dedication to what they do. The film's characters are the saddler, the leather craftsman, the glassmaker, the jeweller and so on.

The documentary was screened at festivals and special events and will be available on www.hermesheartsandcrafts.net.

Cine Joia

Created from the ashes of a 1950's cinema, when it was a meeting point for the intellectuals of the city, Cine Joia (Jewel, in Portuguese) has now been returned to San Paulo

thanks to an extraordinary restoration project. In November 2011, the Music hall opened with a memorable inauguration party, leaving visitors breathless. The project, while
renovating the structure and some of the original materials, created a series of design
innovations that bewilder and amaze the public. The hall offers unexpected points of view:
the slope of the floor, lighting system, and 2D projections on 3D surfaces. A key part of
the concept for the creators of Joia, André Juliani, Facundo Guerra and Lucio Ribeiro who
express themselves in a place that literally moves around music, weather it be rock, jazz,
punk, or MPB.

Veuve Clicquot Polo Classic

The annual Veuve Clicquot Polo Classic played on Governor's Island signifies the start
of the Island's public access season of free events and activities. The polo match is a
free event sponsored by Veuve Clicquot and benefiting Hope Help & Rebuild Haiti (HHRH)
charities. It is an initiative of Urban Zen founded by New York designer Donna Karan. The
location of the match is special because between World War I and World War II polo was
often played on Governors Island and the launch of this free philanthropic event marks
the return to use of this historic Island after nearly 75 years. City dwellers put on their
best polo match attire (hats and all) and head to the Island in large groups to enjoy a day
outdoors; pre-packing picnics or lunching from one of the gourmet food stalls serving
barbeques, sandwiches, salads and more.

Premium Seekers

Comsumption as

- Reflection in a more than traditional world of cultural luxury.
- Elitist choices that confirm their social role.
- The constant search for innovative products and services.

Communication as

- Re-reading in original ways, aspects related to tradition and the narrative of prestige.
- Exclusive messages aimed at the elite of which they feel part.
- Subtle levers of fascination able to highlight their power and their success.

Retail as

- Landscapes that emphasize exclusive and emotional hedonic/hedonistic experiences.
- Places for narration of excellence and brand culture.
- Expressions and recognition of their uniqueness in relation to the purchase experience.

Strategic guidelines

➡ **Propose** exclusivity as a distinctive key in the use of products and services.

➡ **Privilege** cultural aspects in addition to those hedonistic for proposals which must go beyond the simple concept of luxury.

➡ **Highlight** discreetly the ability to select the best.

➡ **Emphasize** the vocation of a brand, in meeting top-of-the-range needs and desires.

➡ **Use** the theme of mastery and unique pieces to transfer its value to unforgettable experiences.

Part Four

The long-lived

The Boomer and Super-Adult generations

The fourth section is dedicated to the over sixties that in many places – for example in Europe and Japan – constitute an increasingly important component of society; not only in purely demographic terms, but also in relation to their strong values and economic influence. For this reason, the definition that we have chosen – that of super-adults – transcends the classic American Boomers label containing at least two of the four generational nuclei that follow. Being a super-adult means not only remaining active within society with their own recognized and respected identity, but also bridging the socio-cultural gap that over the past 30 years seemed hopeless. Indeed, the elderly actually seemed destined for inevitable marginalization, with games of cards at the local bar and long-term hospital care. The changing dynamics of global society appeared to reward youthfulness and isolate the condition of the elderly in a dimension of minimum relevance. Within a few years the situation has completely changed: the arrival of a generation mellowed by the values of freedom, independence, initiative and critical thinking, settled into a new condition created by the violent economic crisis. The long-lived became super-adults because in many cases they became the lifeline for the younger generations of children and grandchildren, who recognized in this generation people they could depend on in terms of economic support, psychological relief and protection in an increasing complicated everyday life.

To better understand the older generation's return to centre stage, a more detailed analysis of the Italian case using data compiled and published by Censis might be useful. Italy is a country with one of the longest living populations in the world. Yet, the condition of seniors has always remained in the responsible and loving hands of the family and a restricted circle of friends, without ever becoming a consideration for social services. The new issue to address is the increasingly worrying demographic imbalance: in Italy for every 100 young people we have 156 elderly people. The answer lies in imagining new services to assist the elderly, but also in facing new challenges in the field of culture and consumption. In the 2015 Censis, analysis discovered that, for the first time, the consumption of couples with an elderly member of the household (aged 65 years and over) was greater than (and not by little: approximately 1,200 euro a year) couples of the younger 18-34 year old category. Also, in the crisis years (2009-2014), the elderly who lived alone increased consumer spending by 4.7% in real terms, while spending of single Millennials dropped (12.4%), as did the average expenditure made by Italian families (11.8%). For 8 out of 10 seniors, family income is today sufficient to cover expenses and for 78% consumption spending increased (18%) or remained stable (60%) during the last twelve months. Optimism in the future reigns: 89% of older people think that, in the coming year, their incomes, savings and consumption are bound to increase (9%) or to remain stable (80%). This helps to explain the positive spending intentions: 1.1 million people aged 65 and over intend to proceed with the purchase of home appliances, 670,000 PCs, smartphones, tablets and other technology products, and 320,000 home furnishings, while around 1 million want to carry out home renovations. Another 530,000 are considering investment in real estate in the next three years. We can therefore speak of the new power of super-adult spending which is confirmed in health, culture, and in support of children and grandchildren. The elderly spend 13 billion euros each year to support their own health and to meet their needs not covered by the public welfare system. An amount which corresponds to almost 40% of Italian private health expenditure, even if the elderly account for just over 20% of the total population. 3.3 million seniors spend 2.7 billion euros a year on training activities for themselves or their family members (perhaps an English course or violin lessons for a grandchild), to which another 960 million euros are added for sports activities. In total, there are 7 million seniors who personally contribute to the wellness of their family, children or grandchildren, and thus funding other people's consumption. The elderly spend 1.9 billion euros each year on domestic help.

The data for Italy is confirmed by comparative analysis with many other advanced economies and allows us to extend the status of super-adults to the 4 nuclei of boomers that we propose in this final section: the Job

Players, the Family Activists, the Pleasure Growers and the Health Challengers.

The Job Players are those who do not give up their professional identity. They are not resigned to retirement, but in many cases have the energy and resources to undertake a second activity, such as following their passion or vocation. For them, work is a way of life more than a source of income. In this nucleus we find all the professional associations related to self-employment that often ensures continuity in their activities with the involvement of children and grandchildren.

Instead, the Family Activists find satisfaction and recognition in supporting their family or peers – friends and relatives – who are in difficulty. They are genuine family activists employing time and resources in activities that complement and enrich their family ménage, defining a new role as, for example, the baby-sitting grandfather.

On the other hand, Pleasure Growers follow the path of mature hedonism, centred on their passions and dedicated to spending time and money fulfilling them without further ado. For them, pleasure trips, knowledge in all its variants, cultured and intelligent consumption, constitute experiences sought after and appreciated for the serenity of mind and judgment in the final stage of their existence.

Finally, the Health Challengers often find themselves having to fight with physical limitations and health problems; they live life as a personal challenge in the face of an intellectual and relational vitality that turns them into resolute fighters, willing to stay for as long as possible in their own homes and rejecting other solutions, for example. In their case, the problem of adequate assistance and care is dramatically raised at an age when independence of spirit no longer corresponds to independence in mobility and autonomy in everyday life.

Job Players

The Job Players nucleus includes many long-living people who are still professionally active or plan to access work again, maybe launching their own independent business. For them, work is a reason to live: more than family or the gratification of consumption. These subjects represent a competent and qualified workforce that is still able to play a role in the professional world, often without the need to defend their job from younger generations. Today, finding new professional placements and imagining their role in transferring talents and competencies is a relevant challenge, particularly if we consider the decisive contribution these long-lived players can make in relating to the elderly. The Job Players – we could also call them the Knights of work – are those long-lived people who strongly display their desire to still take an active part in the professional world, either by staying in or re-accessing the labour market. Many elderly people still want to work not only to have some extra income. In Italy, 3.2 million elderly people still work: more than one million are in regular employment, while more than 2.1 million work occasionally. These are spontaneous declarations that respond to different contractual conditions, presumably also undeclared work. This nucleus is striking due to their courage and initiative. More than 407,000 long-lived people say that they will try launching their own independent activity in the near future. Their desires are well distributed: 230,000 want to launch an artisanal activity, 229,000 a professional activity, and 178,000 a commercial activity.

This reveals a strong desire to remain active, with creative energies that converge into new life projects: 198,000 long-lived people say they want to launch a small company. They are the variation of super-adults that most undermines the stereotypical retired person, who lives in his/her own world, unable to have a open and frank engagement with the outside world and with the needs of other generations. On the other hand, Job Players show a desire to lead an active life, by using their experience and competence to take decisions and responsibilities that have a real effect on the collective decisions of society, which they still feel like an integral part of. The new dignity conferred to the many craftsmen who still continue working, trying to preserve the teaching of practical skills, is one of the roads to relaunch a generation of over-seventy-year-olds that does not accept being marginalized in their families or at the bar. Their daily life and their consumption standards reflect their condition as active, responsible and expert subjects, in the sense of their plentiful accumulated experience, which today can be re-defined and re-proposed intelligently. A patrimony of useful knowledge is created for new generations to perfect their know-how. The dimension of traditional "consumption" is not as relevant to Job Players as being acknowledged as "experts."

Job Players consider environmental and social conditions as a starting point for their original creativity, and transform sustainability and the search for excellence into an alternative and innovative vision. Design partnerships and rigour are the basis for solid relationships of trust. They apply their effort to every sphere of life, from culture, work and leisure, in search of tools that consolidate their worldview. Their transgressive spirit, plurality of thought, and heterogeneity as an intergenerational expressive language, are the tools they use to re-define daily life and its evolution in terms of "future normality." The local and global dimension meet in the various places and manifestations of Job Players' daily lives. In fact, their "global reality" is deeply rooted in the local, in order to enhance the value of the territory, creativity and artisanal traditions.

From the point of view of consumption, Job Players are careful and informed spenders; their attitude is more similar to professional buyers than that of simple consumers. In their case, professionalism in purchasing becomes obsessive: often they influence many other generations and our proud of leading opinion in choosing brands and products. The fields they feel most confident in are; the home, cars, furniture, financial services, and technology in a broad sense, as well as accessories of various kinds.

They favour informative communication with substance, oriented to-wards innovation more than novelties, aimed at clarity, and sustained by substance and practicality. When making purchases – and online – they appreciate a guaranteed price-quality ratio. Human interaction with sales staff or store managers is a must for them, and being constantly updated on the functional and performative features of products is absolutely necessary.

Their point of observation, in any country and culture, always derives from knowledge distilled from their long professional experience, through cultures in various sectors and dimensions of living and working, and is therefore never banal or conventional. They combine technical knowledge about processes with a passion for knowing how to do things well and better than anyone else.

Future professionals: Object regenerators and maintainers

Today, the stories of "individuals," discordant voices, and personal tastes, increasingly become a point of reference for new crafts and renewed pro-fessional activities. The world of consumption is taking on new challenges from the most unusual contexts and from "niches" in order to re-think production processes and dynamics, thereby inventing commercial and business alternatives. New economic systems and models are developed focused on what we could define as tailoring on the one hand, and main-tenance on the other. We are talking about tailors (not fashion designers), embroiderers, craftsmen who know how to interpret the taste of the cus-tomer in a unique way and how to give value to the exceptions (and even defects) of each one. We are in the dimension of value that many Job Play-ers acknowledge as the most important not only in their activity, but also in their way of seeing and experiencing the world.

And we are not only referring to craftsmen who love their activity, but to maintainers, those who repair with good taste and skill (footwear, um-brellas, bags, but also bicycles and electronic equipment), and who seemed destined to inevitably disappear in the era of disposable things. Today, on the other hand, those who know how to regenerate objects and give them a second life seem to be back in vogue and lead a happier and more responsible life. The web, social networks, and the entire digital world have strangely amplified this trend in a paradoxical alliance between in-novation and preservation. Everyone is expecting to be served, spoiled, acknowledged for his or her own passions and needs, and the search for those who can guarantee a service that restores the dignity of used things is becoming a collective obsession. This phenomenon has repercussions for society and the family: grandchildren are once again observing their grandmother's cooking skills or their grandfather fixing and building things with their hands, in order to learn the craft of maintenance and preservation and to invent new and re-discover ancient activities that revive the value of our everyday objects. They are learning discrete forms of caretaking that had been forgotten in recent decades. Any craft capable of giving new life to things will have a future. But as long as trade and the world of professions continue to think only in terms of price and visibility, without facing the bigger issue of maintaining, they will have missed the opportunity of the future.

Maestros Academy, Italy

Job Players represent an extraordinary patrimony of experience, memory, talent, that we will have to learn to appreciate the future. The Korean company Samsung sensed this when it proposed the project "We don't just launch products, we launch people" in Italy, by creating the Maestros Academy, a project in which skilled craftsmen stimulate young people to follow the traditions of Italian craftsmen. At Maestros Academy, users can attend courses taught by five traditional masters. "Samsung's Maestros Academy project is meant to be a starting point to safeguard Italian tradition and pass it on to the new generations," Luca Danovaro, corporate marketing director of Samsung Electronics Italy, explained.

THE EMBLEMATIC CASE STUDIES

Worn Wear Patagonia

Patagonia, an outdoor clothing and accessories company, guarantees that its clothing (reponsibly sourced organic cotton, or merino wool) can last for life. Its repairs facility, located in Reno, is considered to be the largest in North America. Since 2013 the brand has encouraging consumers to repair their old Patagonia garments before buying something new through the project, Worn Wear. In 2015, Patagonia sent the group's Nevada repair department traveling "on the road," with the objective of crossing the country. The Worn Wear Tour started in Ventura, California, on April 2nd, with the intention of spreading a responsible consumption message. Offering their garments repair services and workshops for free, the team stopped at various outlets, coffee shops, town squares and farmers markets.

Fish

Located in Sausalito, San Francisco, is a fresh seafood restaurant with sweeping views of the bay, which has a wide pier available with wooden picnic tables where customers can enjoy a meal and the atmosphere, while learning about sustainable fishing. All ingredients are strictly organic, with a range of fish sourced directly from local fishermen. The menu changes daily depending on what has been caught, and a blackboard behind the counter with handwritten text lists the daily specials. Next to the restaurant, the owners have also opened a fish shop with an office linked to their organization FOCB (Fish Or Cut the Bait, www.focb.org). It is a space commited to "dispel myths and clichés" about the world of fishing, with a clear focus on sustainability.

Anti PowerPoint Party

The Internet becomes a fundamental instrument in proposing new forms of thought and new criteria for the selection of content. Founded by M.Pohem, the Anti PowerPoint Party is an international political party, with it headquarters in Switzerland, in order to attract the greatest possible media attention. The aim is to reduce the negative influence of PowerPoint on conferences and lessons, favouring the development of less linear thought management systems.

Steteco

Steteco is a Japanese brand that created a must have clothing product for the Japanese youth. The winning idea re-proposes, in ultra-fashionable colours and prints, a product of everyday use from traditional Japanese dress: *suteteko* pants made from cotton, are a cross between underwear and trousers for the home and were originally only used by elderly people in informal and domestic situations. This garment, which also has the advantage of helping preserve body temperature, is therefore wearable in different seasons and has quickly become a wildcard youth fashion statement. In this project, functionality, standard and energetic creativity mix in this project, which even in terms of advertising targets the cool youth market.

Job Players

Consumption as

- A control variable to show the younger generations their social value.
- A set of choices oriented towards expertise.
- Everyday experiences of relax complementary to work time.

Communication as

- Sharing of knowledge regarding production processes.
- Rigor in the narrative of products and processes, accurately communicated.
- Care and attention in giving significance to details and finishes.

Retail as

- Places to render tangible the brands projects, sharing goals with clients.
- Involvement in extra-consumption activities with educational objectives related to know-how.
- Markets in which to generate new forms of competent exchange of direct self-production.

Strategic guidelines

- **Offer** targeted and differentiated products and services to give concrete answers to specific problems that require inventive and practical solutions.
- **Contribute** with active tools to raise awareness of the quality of products and production processes.
- **Design** places of exchange and experimentation online and offline, where the brand can enable a constructive dialogue with its users.
- **Consider** as strategic the collaboration between business and civil society to give innovative answers to everyday problems.
- **Support** with concrete and relevant initiatives the self-organized territorial community activities: for example buying groups and social housing.

Family Activists

Family Activists are the children of the Second World War; from an early childhood were used to dealing with daily constraints and financial difficulties. They represent a growing part of the senior population, which especially after the global crisis in 2008, is re-acquiring its role in the family and social life, even in countries where it had been lost altogether. In fact, for these people, leaving the employment market means becoming "full time" grandparents and being actual "supporters" of the family.

Their organizational skills, interest in other people's lives, and skills in listening to the needs of their children and grandchildren, in addition to others who are close to their vital context, make them interesting representatives of a broad consumption of goods and services. They define their social role in terms of proximity: the apartment building, the neighbourhood, the local marketplace, as well as their grandchildren's school and children's home.

Family Activists are active elderly people who are both aware of their own age and the key role they play in the extended family. Their strength is the material and organizational support they provide in daily family management. Some of their priorities are:

- the building a new, shared daily life;
- consumption focused more on their relatives than themselves;
- attention towards care and protection;
- the importance of networks of social solidarity.

Family Activists share the knowledge they have acquired over time at the moment when narrative intersects with know-how: nurturing rituals and traditions with interpretations, arrangements, and personal tastes. The pleasure of being and doing things together stretches as far as an interest in social solidarity networks. Organizational and listening skills, which come from the needs of their children and grandchildren, become valuable talents even beyond the family. Attention for one is understood as an active and constant care for oneself and others, whom they offer their knowledge and practical experience to. In the family, they provide original and functional choices and solutions. For Family Activists, even daily life and family contexts can offer vital and surprising experiences, thanks to a range of enriching services. The home thus becomes an inspiration for values and initiatives even outside the home.

This group of long-lived people is marked by an existential priority we could define as "daily activism." In fact, in their experience, the human, psychological, and cultural contribution is strongly felt as they help their family (and/or in their nearby communities), employing their own resources of time, skills, and money to support other generations as well as dependent peers. These "family activists" are thus re-launching the role of the grandparents for teenagers. The consolidation of this group seems to mark the end of elderly people's marginalisation in family and society in general, in the name of a new active responsibility. This is the group that defines the support of their "descendants" as a vital priority. In Italy, more than 1.5 million elderly people state that they contribute to the family of their children or grandchildren with their own money. All possible forms of support are included in this dimension of "daily activism": from educational support, to more specific cultural and psychological support, and religious devotion. One of the most common forms of activism concerns grandmothers' effort in taking care of their grandchildren. The generational short circuit that risked dying out is thus re-activated. Vertical activism – that is, activism aimed at young generations – is clearly apparent from statistics: more than 3.2 million long-lived people are taking care of their grandchildren, and almost 5.7 million do so from time to time. There is also horizontal activism: more than 972,000 long-lived people are regularly taking care of other elderly people who are not self-sufficient, such as spouses, relatives, but also dear friends.

While in Italy the central role of family in everyone's life and, particularly, in the lives of the elderly, is considered normal; in other countries, such as England or the United States, this is much less obvious. The possibility of re-establishing an emotional bond, albeit for financial or organizational reasons, leads to peculiar life experiences that even give more strength and depth to consumption behaviour. Think, for instance, about the senior population's constantly growing demand for being informed about new technologies. It reflects their desire not to lose touch with new generations of children and grandchildren.

For Family Activists, exiting the labour market means entering their role as "full time" grandparents, as well as being true "supporters" of the family. The time they have available thanks to having left work becomes a vast pool of resources to be placed at the disposal of others, whether they are members of the traditional family or the "extended family" of the neighbourhood, an association, or a social entity with which they feel in tune. The time they make available is precious, because it is qualitatively different from the younger generations: it is a relaxed time, without stress or short-term goals to reach, with the potential of becoming a time for sharing and to educate the youngest for the future.

Apart from being a material resource for the family, Family Activists also become a cultural resource; they are bearers of traditional knowledge of both practices and values. Baking cookies together and listening to stories from the far-away past, are pastimes that grandparents and grandchildren can share, just as much as going to the park or playing cards.

In this sense, there is an interesting cross-over between the growing emphasis towards a soft activism – far removed from the more radical and ideologically biased formulas – and the focus on family bonds. In fact, the family is being transformed from single-parent families to broader forms of extended community: not only are aunts/uncles and cousins once again becoming part of the family core, but also friends and neighbours. In other words, the very concept of proximity is changing and is once again drawing on the logics of pre-industrialized society. In this sense, even the apartment building or the neighbourhood are a pool of new emotional bonds, trust and solidarity. In this framework, Family Activists, with their experience and wisdom about relationships, are an important point of reference.

In the sphere of consumption, attention to price represents an essential pillar, and the logic of gratuitousness takes on the form of emotional exchange: for Family Activists, the possibility of being young again by living vicariously through their grandchildren is their biggest compensation for caring for them, with tangible consequences for their consumption behaviour. Purchasing is almost always a shared experience – if consciously or not – and today we can also detect a regular use of the web in Family Activists encouraged by frequent interaction with younger generations, whether they are their children or grandchildren. The activism of this nucleus has also transformed their role in the family sphere, where they provided financial support and helped in daily activities (baby sitting, assisting grandchildren in their studies), to a consumer activism in a broader sense, with an interest in outlets and farmer markets where they are particularly skilled, and a cultural vocation performed on the territory – for instance, taking part in urban festivals with their children and grandchildren, and in more collective shows, from celebrations in town squares to street theatres.

They no longer make impulse purchases for themselves, but make up for it through purchases and smaller payments of an absolutely "irrational" nature for the younger generations.

Future professionals: Home simplifiers

Simplifying domestic life is appreciated in collective student life as well as in single life, by various members of a family as much as the "digital elderly." This evolution corresponds to a new market and to ancient "crafts," which in the past were absorbed by the extended family or by the "service" staff in charge of the maintenance in the home. Family Activists – who are still very active in the home and in their family's daily life – particularly appreciate anything that can simplify domestic chores, which to them are an essential part of their presence in the home. They represent an important number of people who require domestic services and thus constitute a platform for new job opportunities. From the growing demand for traditional plumbers and electricians, we are moving towards a professionalization of do-it-yourself work and an extension of cleaning services for the home and clothes, with washing and ironing services. The number of people, especially women, who spend their time away from home due to their jobs, is growing exponentially. This requires new flexibility and speed in satisfying the basic needs of domestic life. As a result, entire sectors dedicated to domestic services will become areas of job opportunities, extending the frontiers of a new domestic economy. In the home, in fact, everyone demands service and quality, comfort and innovation. Many stress that the most traditional rites related to cooking or childcare will be re-thought or "amplified" by ground-breaking technological applications: but also that the human dimension of caretaking and assistance, which is becoming increasingly professionalized and will play an important role in this scenario.

Zaarly

Zaarly is an online platform to help select the best home professionals in your area. With one click you can read their references and book gardening services, electricians, plumbers, and cleaning staff. The App allows you to "network" and broadens the exchange between the people demanding and offering domestic services. Bo Fishback, CEO of Zaarly.com, declared that his main goal was to help people earn a living by supporting them to solve domestic problems. With Zaarly you can just earn extra money or develop an actual business activity. Zaarly also provides the service Storefronts, which offers professionals presentation pages with their own "brand" – including photographs, biography, and a description of the service provided and estimated costs – with the purpose of creating a more dynamic relationship.

THE EMBLEMATIC CASE STUDIES

Settimo Cielo, Italia

The Family Activists show themselves to have growing confidence towards advanced technologies, to which children and grandchildren introduce them. Settimo Cielo was born in Settimo Torinese in 2007. The protagonists are ten people over the age of 60 who have created a web based editorial team that manages an urban blog, to comment on, live and re-live the past and present life of the city. The project, developed by the *Osservatorio Scrittura Mutante della Biblioteca Civica Multimediale di Settimo* in collaboration with the Pari-Go Onlus, started life as a training course designed to bring the population closer to multimedia tools and transformed into a collective blog. The scope of the course was to learn how to write online and build a personal and collective identity. The use of the blog as an instrument brings the family activists, who too often having little familiarity with the Internet, back into play. Today, the over 60's of Settimo have given life to a unique and special window into the city for everyone.

Home Food

Home Food is a project sponsored by the Italian Ministry of Agriculture, in collaboration with the University of Bologna and regional authorities. It places strong emphasis on sharing and teaching the cultural values found in homemade food from the region, thanks to the preparation of traditional dishes by housewives from the area. In fact, the association organizes events where it's possible to register as a dinner guest in a real Italian family home. The guest tastes and is exposed to food that is made according to traditional recipes. The hosts are called Cesarine, in homage to the grandmother's and aunts who, historically, were the family chefs. At the beginning of 2012 a group of Cesarine went on tour in the USA, giving traditional homemade Italian cooking lessons in California, Florida and New York.

Becoming Grandma

In the book *Becoming Grandma*, Lesley Stahl, one of the most recognizable journalists in the US, discusses how becoming a grandmother transforms a woman's life. The most vivid and transformative experience of her life was not reporting on the White House, interviewing heads of state, or researching stories for *60 Minutes*. It was becoming a grandmother. She explored how grand mothering changes a woman's life, interviewing friends like Whoopi Goldberg, colleagues like Diane Sawyer, as well as the proverbial woman next door. She speaks with scientists and doctors about physiological changes that occur in women when they have grandchildren; anthropologists about why there are grandmothers in evolutionary terms; and psychiatrists about the therapeutic effects of grandchildren on both grandmothers and grandfathers. In an era when baby boomers are becoming grandparents in droves and when young parents need all the help they can in raising their children, Stahl's book is a timely and heart-warming read that redefines a cherished relationship.

Walgreens Boots Alliance

Walgreens Boots Alliance is a large American pharmacy led by Italian chief executive Stefano Pessina. At the end of 2015 it acquired its rival Rite Aid in a deal valued at $ 17.2 billion that gave rise to a new leader in large-scale drugstore chains in the United States, by uniting two of the three main players in the industry. The new group has at its disposal a network of 13,000 pharmacies in eleven countries. Its presence is primarily concentrated in New York, California, Florida and Texas. Walgreens defines itself as "the greatest destination in the United States and Europe for pharmaceutical retail, health and everyday life" and proposes a format that combines drugstore, convenience store and pharmacy as part of a true temple of health and well being for all. The groups' advertising offers a careful mix of products and services attentive to social phenomena, which varies according to the location. In the shops, the sale of drugs and medical advice is always guaranteed, due to the presence of a medical practice open 24 hours a day. The in-store atmosphere is engaging, mainly because the furnishings are far removed from those typical of a regular pharmacy.

Family Activists

Consumption as

- Reassurance by simplifying everyday choices.
- Search for products and services to be enjoyed with grandchildren.
- Predilection for offers that have the added value of solidarity.

Communication as

- Need for simple and direct information.
- The importance of family and friends as a privileged sources of information.
- Progressive approach to the world of the web and its relational potential.

Retail as

- Possibility to build stable, reliable relations over time with those who sell.
- Use of what the territory offers: farmers' markets, country fairs, factory outlets, cultural events.
- Constant pursuit of opportunities with the best price/quality ratio.

Strategic guidelines

- **Select** products and experiences-services that simplify daily life from an intergenerational perspective.
- **Propose** sales spaces that also act as collectors for community needs, particularly felt by this generation.
- **Create** opportunities and spaces where people can express their passions, promoting shared rituals.
- **Stimulate** initiatives and organized meetings where men and women of all ages can approach new themes and practices and learn from others.
- **Create** occasions and communicative strategies in which the seniors can demonstrate their competence and experience, playing the role of "masters" for other generations.

Pleasure Growers

"The moment has finally come to enjoy myself"

(Over 70 year olds, males and females)

This generational nucleus refers to those long-lived people who, once they have freed themselves from the burdens of adult life, choose – and have a chance – to have a full life, rich in projects and gratifying activities for their own physical and psychological wellbeing. They are not only new consumers, but also re-designers of their lives, which could be a social reference for the elderly of the future. Pleasure Growers dedicate a lot of their time and energy to relationships, not only to subjective consumption. This is the group of long-lived people that re-design their own life based on their interests, sensitivity, expectations, and make their own quality of life a top priority, expressing a mature and substantial hedonism. In Italy, for instance, they are the advanced tip of those 84% of elderly people who assess their lives positively and those 66% of Italians who are not afraid of growing old. One of the activities they desire most is traveling: in Italy, as many as 151,000 elderly people travel abroad regularly, and about 2.9 million do so from time to time. They cultivate the small pleasures of life with determination.

Pleasure Growers, especially in the west, represent a group of "mature vitals" who do not accept the typical behaviour of the Third Age, and who seek and create experiences in line with contemporary values. Daily experimentation, mental exploration, tangible innovation, these are the keywords characterizing one of the basic values of this generational nucleus. The higher average life expectancy determines the "shifting" of age groups and the statistical growth of a generation which, once re-generated, is re-discovering a new position for itself in society, new potential (financial, social, and cultural) and a lot of "empty space" to use it.

For some time already, countless scientific and sociological studies, both national and international – like a research study from the Swedish University of Göteborg – have posited that sex in old age is not a rare phenomenon, but rather quite regular and natural, both in and outside of matrimony (seven elderly people out of ten declare they have regular sexual relationships). The generation that experienced the first sexual revolution as adults is now breaking down this last taboo, supported by an increased care for the body, which, in the last fifteen years, has improved the over-70-year-olds' physical condition and performance.

In the 1960s, Great Britain and the US – the countries in which Pleasure Growers emerged first – produced a large number of individuals who "have made history" and who are coming back today as Masters in the collective imagination of the third millennium: in fashion, music, design, and style. From Mick Jagger and Bob Dylan, to Vivienne Westwood and Joan Baez, from Paul Smith to Twiggy, and from the Beatles to David Byrne, we are today experiencing a new renaissance of the avant-gardes. By re-proposing their original work, the stimuli these artists create is more mature and accessible yet equally intense.

The phenomenon of Pleasure Growers has extended beyond the borders of the Anglo-Saxon world to other developed countries, both in the Western world (from France to Spain) and in Japan. The countries, which in the sixties and seventies experienced commercial and cultural development, are today showing a particular sensitivity to the utopias of the past, that endure and improve as they age (like good wines). These are transformed into fuel for visions that are asserting themselves more and more on a universal scale. From the most advanced sustainable cities, to the underground visions of Wakamatsu Koji, up to the organic sensitivity of two great old guys like Frank Gehry and Rafael Moneo.

The courage of those who no longer need to compete or prove themselves is the best trait of a generation that has a lot to offer but is still demanding: this generational nucleus has the clearest ideas of all about its future. The assertion of this group implies the definition of an entirely new and re-generated style of consumption: informal, young, and energetic. In other cases, the superfluous – like the game – becomes the main driver of their experience. Simplifying means possessing techniques, taste and knowledge to recognize the useless and redundant aspects of existence. Sharing life experiences is another priority for this group of subjects. Among Pleasure Growers the awareness that "free space" can give you the chance to increase your creativity and visionary capacity is spreading. In the field of consumption, the importance this group attributes to comfort, playfulness and to the value of life experiences orients it mainly towards the industries of tourism, services, leisure, and domesticity.

They are planners and leave nothing to chance. In the US, they even organize their own funeral, reading through catalogues and choosing their tombstones, flower arrangements, and the wood of the coffin well ahead of time. With their advance payments, they have guaranteed the success of funeral companies which, like the market leader Service Corp, owe 30% of their revenues to funeral expenses paid in advance, and predict an annual growth of 2% precisely in relation to the Boomers.

For each one of these fields, products need to offer simplification, playful learning, emotional gratification, and emotion. A great revolution in this sense comes from the world of hi-tech design, which is increasingly oriented towards creating easy to use objects that offer immediate functionality, without compromising on comfort and design.

Pleasure Growers, therefore, are a group of vital elderly people who, despite their age, try to have happy experiences. "The moment has finally come to enjoy myself, maybe by doing something I have never done before" – this is the motto of this group, for which growing old is seen as an opportunity to have more time for themselves and, above all, for everything they have always dreamed of, but never had enough time for. Undoubtedly, traveling represents the most pleasurable experience. Often their travels are studded by a series of small rituals that also lie in their choice of hotels and restaurants, aside from the locations they visit. Informal, young, in some cases ironic and experimental, the new traveling seniors are in search of experiences to re-discover, maybe taken from their own youth and filtered through their mature age. The relationship with the family is a potentially emotional environment for them, but very often they have remained alone – divorced or widows/ers – and find a possible pool of new company in social occassions.

Their search for authenticity is expressed by attempting to find the essence of things and distil basic values from experiences. They establish emotional bonds with objects and places: the Swedish company, Rosa Bussarna, operates in different countries around the world, organzing tours on its famous pink caravans. These big pink buses are typical of this service, and offers itineraries only for "young seniors" who show an adventurous desire to re-live their backpacking years. Pleasure Growers are interested in all those places, objects, and contexts that allow them to transform their journey into an experience of intelligent hedonism, based on pleasure and quality experiences. At the heart of their experience we find renewed time for themselves, a different way of seeing their future, freed from ordinary commitments and duties and moving towards a definition of other experiences and forms of sharing. The time and experiences they engage in are used to enhance their personal awareness. With them, it is possible to recover a long-term vision and re-generate values to believe in.

The focus on their own wellbeing, from all perspectives, dictates their daily choices of products and contexts able to nourish their health and personal happiness. Being comfortable with their body thus becomes a delicate and crucial life project. Within this framework of surprising re-discovery there is also a certain enjoyment of themselves, beyond the traditional stereotypes related to their age. It is a joyful conquest, where even relationships enjoy a new sense of time and pleasure. For Pleasure Growers it is important that the entertainment spaces, apart from offering entertaining and recreational experiences, are also able to propose cognitive contexts and stimuli, allowing them to explore their personal interests.

Future professionals: Elderly travel assistant

In many cases, the Web has made the services of travel agencies and tour operators obsolete. An entire industry has suffered under the devastating impact of web portals like Booking.com or TripAdvisor, which, contrary to predictions about the disintermediation of this business model for the new millennium, have proven to represent the absolute zenith of a business model in which nothing is produced and no material service is provided. Rather, this model is designed to further the aggregation of data and select commercial companies to be re-distributed on the Web in terms of indications, suggestions, and combinations that are mixed for the end customer. In fact, being able to define or manage reservations on-line in real time leads us towards a model in which the diktat is to simplify purchasing decisions, optimize value for sellers, and simulate convenience for buyers. All this proves to be particularly relevant in the segmented area of travel planning, proposing tourist experiences for groups of long-lived people who often exhibit values and behaviours similar to Pleasure Growers. Lovers of traveling, they hunt for gratifying experiences and are willing to place themselves in the hands of agencies that offer bespoke services. In many cases, their priority is not financial convenience, but the guarantee of safety and intelligent company in their adventures around the world. The typical "group trip" which Pleasure Growers seek, could thus be transformed into a memorable and shared experience in which the cultural competence of the guides, the reliability of information about places to visit, and the organization of "special experiences" at the reach of the most long-lived customers, could become decisive elements in traveling. The new profession of Elderly Travel Assistants – addressed exclusively at over-70-year-old tourists – could therefore help these customers avoid queues and long waiting times at passport controls, make it easier to choose restaurants, guarantee quick and safe health assistance in case of need, and thereby dissipate the typical anxiety and concerns of this age group for subjects who also love to have new travel experiences.

Baby Boomers Social Club

The Baby Boomers Social Club in Portland is a club located in the Red Lion, a complex known as the "Top of Cosmo." It's a place where you can organize events and dances – with music ranging from the '50s to the '70s, and sometimes even the '80s – and where old friends meet or new friendships are born. The website declares: "we've left our inhibitions and poses in High School, now all we have left is having fun!" The Club published the *Business Guide of Boomers*, which advertises its sponsors, lists the club's activities and noteworthy information, such as, which friendships or couples have been created in the club. Also, there is a strong desire to be part of the community and support local companies. Many members are entrepreneur boomers who have launched their own businesses, and one of the clubs offers mutual support among members.

THE EMBLEMATIC CASE STUDIES

ShapeUp Gym

ShapeUp Gym in Milan is a gym that offers individual or small group courses where each person is guided with great care and professionalism. The system is planned and differentiated for each different age group, from children to seniors who can take part in Pilates and gentle exercise. This is a place of "active wellbeing" which offers an open

environment for friends to share personalised services, but also facilitates intergenerational dynamics. It is not uncommon for grandmothers and grandchildren to visit this gym
together to take part in physical activity at the same time and in the same spaces. The
convenience of having a single place where they can visit for Personal and Family Welfare
benefits seniors increasingly occupied with actively caring for their grandchildren.

Bauputang Tea House, China

All over the world the Pleasure Growers constitute not only a consumer target, but also
the collective memory of experience that will be increasingly appreciated in the market
of the future. Set within a park in north Beijing, Baoputang is a tearoom with a private
kitchen offering the best experience around the ritual of drinking tea. Zi Tong, founder
and pioneer of this venture, along with his business partner Zhang Zhi Yong, personally
select organic tea from Fujian and Yunnan, establishing a strong relationship with local
farmers, as well as exploring remote areas to find the best product. Tong also designs
and produces a limited number of pieces of tea ware for tea lovers, in collaboration with
expert ceramic craftsmen. This venue thus reinterprets the ancient tea tradition in an
ideal space for the mind and the senses.

Advanced Style

The peculiarity of Advanced Style, a blog created in 2008 focused on the clothing style
of New Yorkers, is dedicated exclusively to the over 70, reaching in some cases those
over 90. Ari Seth Cohen, the young founder, explains that the elderly (naturally not all!)
show a deep awareness of their own style, which is a global lifestyle linked to clothing,
as well as reflecting personal details. Their greater experience linked to a "golden age" of
fashion makes these subjects the respected style icons and examples for the future, even
by the young. Attentive listening and the building of trusting relationships are the basis
of Cohen's observational work, which delicately captures the sentimental tale of life that
often accompanies the photos.

Flos 50

To celebrate its 50th anniversary, Flos launched an iPad application. The app was not
simply a catalogue, but a journey through the history of the brand, an "activator of memory" that re-proposes the emotions, passions and even the sensorial appeal of historic
Flos products. Piero Gandini, the CEO of Flos, collaborated with writer and journalist Stefano Casciani and Turkish photographer Ramak Fazel in creating the history of the family
and company. The app offers a detailed chronological sequence of events, full of archived
images of the people who started the company, as well as sketches, prototypes, games,
products and videos of the production processes.

Pleasure Growers

Consumption as

- Emotional gratification through products that become daily partners.
- Food, tourism and body care as personal and shared priorities.
- Life experiences oriented towards an intelligent playful hedonism.

Communication as

- Liberation from the stereotypes of old age.
- Search for an ironic and fun point of view.
- Enhancement of their own experience and their own personal uniqueness.

Retail as

- A collector which meets the need for sharing among peers.
- Place where to deepen their passions, often ritualising.
- Space based on competence and discretion, which is demanded by the sales staff.

Strategic guidelines

- **Consider** consumption as an important source of stimulus to add value to everyday life.
- **Propose** offers of "key in hand" products and services, with the possibility of calling on experts and consultants.
- **Encourage** the desire to freely express their dynamism and the pleasure of getting back into play.
- **Start** from the sense of belonging, from the roots and the genius loci to launch large-scale projects, between communication and culture.
- **Tell** the identity, the history, the evolution of a brand through the identity and the life stories of people.

Health Challengers

"I ask not only for assistance"

(75-90 year olds, males and females)

This is the group of seniors for whom health is a daily challenge. We are here referring to the growing number of elderly people who live in a condition of reduced independence and have become dependent on others (more than two million people in Italy). It is a condition which cannot be restricted to the – albeit necessary – medical and nursing assistance. Health Challengers often find themselves contending with physical and health limitations as a personal challenge, in comparison to their intellectual and relational liveliness that transforms them into indomitable fighters who want, for instance, to live in their own homes as long as possible, refusing other solutions. In their case, the profound problem of appropriate assistance and care arises, at an age in which independence of spirit does not necessarily correspond to independence in mobility and daily life.

We will not go into detail about the phenomenological characteristics of this nucleus, which are, as usual, summed up in the statistics. Instead, to conclude this journey through the generations, we will launch an appeal concerning the dignity of the Health Challengers, who often find themselves alone with their relatives facing the insurmountable difficulties of their condition. For them, consumption takes on the fundamental role of measuring their health: i.e. it becomes an important psychological goal to integrate into their days – which are often very repetitive – consisting of small pleasures and personal gratifications within a framework of daily limitations. Their very particular condition as ConsumAuthors requires a simplification of services, which is combined with an ever-greater spec-ificity of products: the market should in this sense create a pool of possi-ble solutions to solve daily problems of health and mobility. In particular, even the world of communication should guarantee the constant support of information about their specific needs and prove its capacity to create a warm relationship based on assistance and consultancy for these frail subjects who are nonetheless determined to be listened to and understood. We should therefore build stable and reliable relationships with this gen-erational nucleus throughout the remainder of their life, for instance, by frequently offering proximity with home care services.

The direction to be taken is that of enhancing the ability of each in-dividual; both people living in residential homes, which in Italy have a potentially expandable market, and those who choose to stay in their own home. Everyone should be guaranteed more care in social terms, which not only includes the need for renewed retirement homes, but also involves new models of individual or collective living. The dependent elderly have very diverse conditions from a financial, psychological, physical, as well as social and cultural point of view. For all, the daily challenge is how to con-tend with the limitations their health imposes on them. In this condition of life we need to re-think assistance, moving from a "depriving" standard to more articulated forms of support. The Italian figures, in this case, are enlightening: as much as 65% of elderly people request new forms of assistance to improve, for instance, their lack of independence outside the home. Often, the challenge also includes considerations that are deeply rooted their daily experience: for instance, sidewalks and roads are indicat-ed by 37.1% of over-65-year-olds as not very functional and inadequate for the elderly population. Then, the problem of permanent assistance emerg-es: the solution of the retirement home for dependent people is liked only by 39.7% of Italians and should, in any case, be more oriented towards social integration. We will stop here, considering that much more could be said about these issues, with the risk, however, of moving too far away from the focus of this book.

Future professionals: Angels of Care

As has already been noted in the previous sections, in the future we will have to increasingly create jobs in which human beings still have a relevant advantage over machines: the jobs that require empathy, creativity, and the ability of taking care of others. Jobs in which people need to be motivated and assisted with human sensitivity, but also professional roles in which you need to know how to listen and take care of others. Or professions that revolve around the ethical values of health and protection: this is also why, when we propose robotics as an advanced form of assistance for the elderly, we make the typical mistake of those who know machines and the most cutting-edge technology well, but not the human psyche. In fact, Health Challengers – who, as we have seen, are destined to make up an ever-growing part of society – will demand the human touch and not only cold technological efficiency.

It is easier for computers to solve problems of immense complexity than to move in a non-repetitive way, orienting themselves in a room, but above all, to take care of a human being and guarantee their safety and psychological balance. There are many jobs, from caretakers for the elderly to hi-tech nurses that have these characteristics, and will consequently experience a big boom in future years. In Italy and Europe generally, we are aware of how fast our population is aging and of the fact that we will need to conceive caretaking services or services of daily physical and psychological support, and sanitary assistance. In this view, a particular role is played by technologies built to monitor health and improve caretaking.

Technology will enter our lives increasingly in the future, but we will need competent professionals to interpret it with less effort in order to free time and energy for our affections and personal passions. As such, the last barrier between the control of our bodies and technological devices will break down. But this will not translate into a loss of jobs because soft technologies to control our health and physical shape will be governed and interpreted by a new group of health specialists, different from the traditional figure of the doctor. We will thus witness one more example of integration between the *human touch* (the care provided by people) and the *tech touch* (monitoring physical conditions by means of wearable technology, such as bracelets that will function as personal trainers, food consultants, and "hi-tech caretakers"), capable of reading our key lifesigns to notify the emergency room and prevent illnesses.

Pillpack

Pillpack is a service that reinvents pharmacies in the US by innovating their management and relational processes and making the activities of the various players involved easier: including the pharmacist, the physician, and, above all, the patient. The son of second-generation pharmacists, the founder, TJ Parker, became aware over time of the difficulties that many patients were having in regularly taking their medicine, as well as of pharmacists' failure in offering support to that effect. He thus designed a service that went beyond selling drugs with an assistance service, now present in over 40 states. Today, prescribed drugs are delivered to patients' homes in packages that state the specific details of consumption. Pillpack's pharmacists manage the supplies for each patient in order to avoid missing a dose of medication. The automated management of every stage leaves doctors and pharmacists more time to converse with their patients.

THE EMBLEMATIC CASE STUDIES

SensFloor

The German company Future-Shape has developed a system of sensors like a textile carpet that can be installed under PVC floor coverings, carpet or laminate, making large scale monitoring possible. SensFloor detects any type of movement on the floor, it is able to understand when people are standing or lying down, and can distinguish between people and other objects, such as liquid spills. The detected signals are sent in real time to a control unit. In health care facilities, this surface could detect when patients leave their beds or if they have fallen and need immediate assistance.

Urban Zen Foundation

"I have spent all my life dressing people, now I want to address them." With these words Donna Karan, one of the great ladies of fashion, explained her project Urban Zen Foundation. It aims to increase self-awareness and wellbeing through inter-cultural exchange, and the introduction of practices and therapies such as yoga and reiki to the west. For this reason, the foundation funds training projects for doctors and nurses who provide rehabilitation care to patients in hospitals (UZIT); manages courses for inter-cultural workers in universities; organizes, through the Urban Zen Foundation, international events and forums, attended by celebrities sensitive to the issue, including Bill Clinton, Richard Gere, the Dalai Lama and Hugh Jackman.

Argento Vivo

The desire for wellbeing is ageless, so Piscine of Vicenza recently proposed a series of activities – including swimming, water aerobics and gymnastics in the pool and the gym – to those over sixty, designed and targeted to the needs of the elderly and at special rates. Argento Vivo is the new program developed for health and wellness whose members are no longer particularly young, but want to keep active. The objective is to reinforce breathing, muscles and posture, gradually improving mental and physical balance.

Nestlé Zhonglaonian Naifen

Nestlé, appropriating the Chinese tradition of "premium gift packages," has created Nestlé Zhonglaonian Naifen as "heartfelt wishes of good health." It is a milk powder, enriched with probiotics "imported from Switzerland," calcium, and brown sugar; it is without additives and emphasizes the property of lowering cholesterol levels. This product is perfect as a gift when visiting older people; traditionally in China, one brings fruit, ginseng or other products from traditional medicine. Nestlé Zhonglaonian Naifen is one of the few products packed and sold in a supermarket that has the right nutritional properties and *premium* quality, making it a suitable choice for such occasions.

Health Challengers

Consumption as

- Important psychological element for the integration of small pleasures and personal satisfaction in a context of everyday limitations.
- Dimension in which the simplification of services is added to the specificity of products.
- Container of possible solutions to mitigate everyday problems in health and mobility.

Communication as

- Constant support of information towards very specific needs.
- Ability to maintain a warm relationship full of help and advice for vulnerable people, eager to be heard and understood.
- Life simplification for users and family members, strongly orientated towards problem solving.

Retail as

- Possibility to build stable, reliable relations over time with those who sell.
- Use of the territorial offers with home delivery.
- Constant search of opportunities with the best price/quality ratio.

Strategic guidelines

- **Evaluate** with more attention the relevance of a nucleus that grows and that in a few years will constitute a relevant market also from the point of view of its size.
- **Imagine** easy to use 'smart' products that offer immediacy of function without sacrificing comfort and design.
- **Give** dignity to a nucleus that appears linked to specific requirements and would appreciate more attention from the market.
- **Reason** in terms of problem solving not only in respect of Health Challengers, but also of family members who often constitute the inevitable boundary.
- **Apply** the wonders of new technology (from sensors to the analysis of Big Data) to alleviate the fragile condition of this generational nucleus.

Conclusions.
From representation to recognition,
arriving at gratitude

The analysis conducted to date has been entirely dedicated to changes in people, following the thread of trends and generations. We have tried to tackle the equation that everyone is trying to solve: what are the new behaviours, values and logics that will shape society and the market of the future?

What to us seems certain is the definitive end to the economic parameters of exchange, marginal costs but also those practices based on the central role of capital and means of production. Instead, the spontaneous potential of collective intelligence emerges without it ever being imagined (Marx[1] had intuited it in *Grundrisse* when talking about general intelligence – unfortunately it fell on deaf ears...). This book has proposed a new logic of recognition that constitutes the definitive end to communication understood as presentation, or worse representation, as we have until now understood it. People no longer wish to be represented: politically or in exclusively material terms and/or for economic interests. They instead wish, above all to become agents of change and for this be recognized, feeling unique with their character and their unique nature as citizens and as ConsumAuthors. As Filippo La Porta writes "There exist many ways of being in the world, but there is also one potentially shared, verifiable, and its no longer someone else to tell us, an expert or a priest. Today we all know that the truth – a common truth, relative but strong, tangible – exists somewhere and that, perhaps for the first time in Western history, everyone has the tools and the ability to recognize."[2] Everyone can actually do it, and

---

[1] Karl Marx, *Grundrisse der Kritik der Politischen Ökonomie* (*Fundamental Criticism of Political Economy*), Marx-EngelsLenin Institute, Moscow, 1939-41.
[2] La Porta, *op. cit.* p.166.

this implies control over their own lives, unimaginable just a few years ago, and makes the media's influence less powerful and its ability to report more strategic. It means abandoning the pyramid of visibility, which for fifty years has characterized consumption in modern society and climbing the pyramid of credibility, which today represents advancement. At the base of the first we find communication, understood as the ability to deliver persuasive messages, sometimes hidden or subliminal, that respond to the never contradicted logic: advertising is the soul of commerce. At the base of the second pyramid we find relation: a logic impossible to adopt if we do not accept the feedback of comparison. This means focusing once again on value-labour which is transformed into value-knowledge-labour and that deeply disrupts the mechanisms of industrial capitalism and finance. Jeremy Rifkin[3] in *The Zero Marginal Cost Society* and Paul Mason[4] in *Postcapitalism* – even if in a different way – explain this very well. The soul becomes the best publicity for commerce.

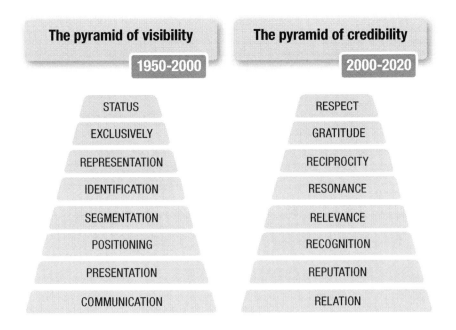

The pyramid of visibility	The pyramid of credibility
1950-2000	2000-2020
STATUS	RESPECT
EXCLUSIVELY	GRATITUDE
REPRESENTATION	RECIPROCITY
IDENTIFICATION	RESONANCE
SEGMENTATION	RELEVANCE
POSITIONING	RECOGNITION
PRESENTATION	REPUTATION
COMMUNICATION	RELATION

[3] Jeremy Rifkin, *The Zero Marginal Cost Society: The Internet of Things, the Collaborative Commons, and the Eclipse of Capitalism*, Palgrave Macmillan, New York, 2014.
[4] Mason, *op. cit.*

From communication to relation

The terms communication and relation might seem synonymous and, in the televised age of our social history, they almost were. All that was important and worthy of attention in people's lives seemed destined to be transformed into communication and/or television information. Each relation, each thought or project seemed destined to pass through the filter of the screen in order to be "real." Everything on TV received the stigma of being the only "true" reality. Everything was true if it appeared on TV: the exact opposite of what is happening today, when television subtracts credibility from a fact or information. Everything else became mere personal opinion, relative and questionable. The five-minutes of television fame imagined by Andy Warhol as a measure of personal identity have long represented the emblematic trademark of this phase. A phase in which visibility (better if televised) prevailed over everything. The most extreme point of this phase, the culmination of the collective imaginary from which it then began to recede, was the invention of the Big Brother TV format, and the unconditioned explosion of reality shows which for ten years colonized the global imagination at all levels. We all still see the lines of thousands of people of all ages, queued for hours waiting for an audition that could maybe give them a second life, a real one, through a simple TV presence. Not so much on TV to do or say anything, but simply to "be there." Today, however, the only real things come from friends and acquaintances, or at least from the "live" dimension enshrined as the only one that matters, measurable even in its economic value, as seen with the success of live performances by artists that people pay handsomely to see. Here it is possible to mark the difference between communication (the generic meaning of a message) and the relationship (made up of an exchange of information and/or live experiences, with the necessary presence of feedback).

From loyalty to gratitude

For a few decades the world of communication was successfully organized through the construction of a message with the goal of reaching the greatest number of people through emotions or structured information. The main goal was to create loyalty, namely the unconditional acceptance of the content of the message and acquired customs in the brand's language.

Emulative nature and human mirroring has transformed this strategy into a powerful asset for both marketing management and corporate communication, which have adopted methods of communication that are as persuasive and repeated as much as possible, creating message discipline not so concerned with adhering to reality (nor the authenticity of life) but "symbolic" and "representative" resistance.

Loyalty thus corresponded to a more or less articulated expectation of a customer-consumer reacting positively to a real or symbolic brand's ability to respect the promises in its communication, and responding appropriately to its demands and desires that it has created. In this dimension the attitude of the consumer is almost passive; they seem to react in an almost instinctive way to the demands of companies, often large multinationals able to produce messages powerful enough to shape the collective imagery. Instead, a completely different dynamic is fuelled by gratitude. Not surprisingly we speak of recognition within personal relationships between friends, and almost never in relationship between brands, companies and consumers. Gratitude would seem to be a feeling limited to the most intimate and private relations, but in the relational dimension this proves to be an effect and not a cause. In fact, gratitude is triggered in response to a particularly generous but unexpected behaviour. We are grateful to someone when they surprise or move us with a "special" act of care and affection towards us: something that was not expected and that in this way expresses its power. The brands, to which we are grateful, are those that in the course of our experience have given us something unexpected, changing lives and becoming memorable. In gratitude, therefore, we find a major psychological element that can hardly be planned around a table, and that instead is almost always the result of radical innovation and not of incremental innovations. For this we cannot follow the path of loyalty, in the sense of satisfying the needs of the consumer and their expectations, but should surprise and transform them. The brand *par excellence* that built its reputation on producing gratitude was Apple with its own master of ceremonies, Steve Jobs. Using technology it unexpectedly transformed the way we work, listen to music, read, write and communicate. In Italy, something similar happened with Adriano Olivetti and Olivetti but in a different way, with Armani's de-constructed jackets that changed the concept of elegance. Or with the Vespa, Nutella and other iconic products and brands, which have, not surprisingly, become part of the history of Italy's consumer culture.

Gratitude is thus the evolutionary leap of relation, compared with loyalty that still belongs to the traditional communication pyramid.

From status to respect

In a society dominated by communication and image, what counts is the status of each individual, as the French sociologist Pierre Bourdieau brilliantly demonstrated in the 70's, with his in-depth study on the standing of social classes, *La distinction*[5]. In fact, status marked its own socio-economic condition through the representation of codes and strict hierarchical symbols, to which brands, products and even individual objects participated – as recounted in 1968 by Jean Baudrillard in *Le Système des objets*[6] and represented a code in terms of social prestige. Today, now that objects communicate with each other, in the dimension of the Internet of things, the previous system of symbols that defined the status of each object is no longer relavent. It is no longer status that matters, but the dignity of each individual, as easily traceable on the Web as reputation measured by powerful algorithms. The normality of each individual is made up of exceptions that can be measured and evaluated, while measuring the value of uniqueness makes job interviews obsolete. All we want to know and understand about someone is easily traceable with the help of the digital world and the "heresphere," which is no longer an "other" or parallel dimension (no one talks of cyberspace) but is our reality – here and now. In this new dimension, status is not relevant and the need for respect takes over: of oneself, of others, of creatures that have become too fragile to withstand the pressure of external judgment or the manipulation of advertising. In the transition to an authentic relationship with the world, awareness and responsibility to the truth becomes necessary.

Recognition passes through human touch, built on psychic and emotional logics that cannot be delegated to third parties. Life lived in the first person is also (but not only) the narcissistic obsession with repeated and permanent selfies, but gradually transforms into the control of their life condition, through being a citizen, consumer, social and relational subject.

---

[5] Pierre Bourdieu, *La distinction. Critique sociale du Jugement*, Minuit, Paris, 1979.
[6] Jean Baudrillard, *Le Système des objets: la consommation des signes*, éd. Gallimard, Paris, 1968.

All of this happens in real time memory that increasingly marginalises the classic requirements of status and relations as traditional components of power: politics, institutions, and money become increasingly irrelevant. For the ConsumAuthors, 100 likes on Facebook (recognition) is more important than paying 100 Euros to enter a trendy nightclub (status). The logics of relevance and therefore also resonance and responsibility change, up to reciprocity and gratitude that strengthen self-respect. It is also because of this that associations/groups not only risk seeing their image becoming highly compromised, but something worse: absolute irrelevance.

The desperate attempt to climb the pyramid of credibility created by loyalty through the traditional techniques of marketing and promotion, appears doomed to failure: In fact, these are consistent with the logic of visibility, where positioning, representation of interests, segmentation, identification, exclusivity and status, count more than recognition. As soon as the client can willingly do without the old armoury of communication, it turns to renewed forms of relationship. What really matters is real life, unexpected passions, deep affections to share (trust & sharing), tastes and personal passions that outweigh social status (unique & universal) and therefore the timeliness of services (quick & deep), the transparency of processes and their traceability (crucial & sustainable). From this need we can no longer escape and those who accept the challenge will receive huge benefits. The Web is eroding the functioning and legitimacy of the market system, but we will have to be ready for this radical change.

In the definition and recognition of ourselves and others, the new dynamics between digital life and real life become decisive. In this book we have proposed generational examples for this new situation: children (Lively Kids) and teens (Expo-Teens) who absorb the stimuli of the digital world like sponges and release them with the freshness and vitality that comes with their age. The intuitive use of digital devices becomes their trademark and the emulation of adult behavioural patterns reaches levels unthinkable only a few years ago. This makes it very difficult for companies to adapt and meet their expectations. Their reaction rate and spontaneous intelligence combine with the lack of filters typical of youth, transforming teenagers into often-merciless mirrors of adult's inability to produce new consumption stimuli for them.

This means that it is necessary to regenerate marketing, communication and retail towards reciprocity, only made possible by the new digital world with its versatility and cognitive energy, allowing companies to engage and excite millions of teens that are used to handling smartphones with ease. As Mason writes "Non-market forms of production and exchange exploit the basic human tendency to collaborate which has always existed but at the margins of economic life. This is more than just a rebalancing between public goods and private goods: it is a whole new and revolutionary thing. The proliferation of these non-market economic activities is making it possible for a cooperative, socially just society to emerge"[7].

On the opposite side we find a group of long-lived over sixty year olds, like the Pleasure Growers. They have ever more resources, energy and culture to face the challenges of the future, but are frequently not considered worthy of attention by public administrations, or by marketing or communication. They often become accomplices and allies of their grandchildren, because they know how to acknowledge them through affective channels. In the middle we have generations on the verge of a nervous breakdown who are forced to re-invent themselves (the CreActives) or who chase the already expired dream of conforming to a model of normality that no longer exists, as in the case of the New Normals. In this game it becomes strategic to understand the new performance requirements in order to recognize and be recognized.

The difficulty in following the strategy of reciprocity is in the subtle understanding of the character and mood of the ConsumAuthors, that can manifest strong cohesion but also profound annoyance in cases where the delicate threshold of intimacy is exceeded. Communication only becomes inviting if it proves capable of moving on the fine line of confidence, discretion and light touch. The first person singular meets the first person plural, and the biography of the individual fits magically into a collective history. The singularity of "I" – amplified and made public through digital technology – coincides more with an "us" in which the identity of the individual overlaps with the groups. In this context, organizations (be they companies or associations), can afford to call, convoke and even mobilize people, provided they show a level of involvement comparable to what is being requested. It is not enough to notify and inform their audience. The call must be individual and sincere, but also touching and engaging, in the deepest sense of etymology. It must solicit gratitude. In fact, etymology reveals that to "move" not only means "disturb," but also "move with,"

---

[7] Mason, *op. cit.*

"put in motion"; as in the case of Federica Fedele who, in dealing with her son's illness, succeeded together with her husband in mobilizing both the scientific and business world. The ultimate goal of this common movement is to "involve," which literally means to "wrap together." The act of convocation can be launched both by companies and individuals, but must always move in unison, transforming a request into a shared action. Only in this way can the virtuous chain of relations, made possible by relevance, translate into mutual recognition, and into the best cases of gratitude. Respect for one and all is still at the top of the pyramid, the *conditio sine qua non* that underpins the entire process. In the coming years the key elements of communication will be "wealth" and "speed," namely the ability to generate content, stories, and meaningful paths, able to reach specific people through different channels and with increasing effectiveness and diminishing disturbance. These stories and tales should be true! A variant of the Quick & Deep paradigm that we could rename Quick & True. Stimulating, timely and authentic: just like the new ConsumAuthors who – sooner or later – will ultimately take power.